Short Introduction to VAISṆAVISM

other recent books from Cosmo Publications . . .

Short Introduction to VAISNAVISM

BY

Subodh Kapoor

Chief Editor
THE HINDUS. Encyclopaedia of Hinduism, in 5 volumes
THE BUDDHISTS. Encyclopaedia of Buddhism, in 5 volumes
Encyclopaedia of Indian Heritage, in 90 volumes
Encyclopaedia of Vedic Philosophy, in 9 volumes
Encyclopaedia of Indian Philosophers, in 9 volumes
The Indian Encyclopaedia, in 25 volumes

COSMO PUBLICATIONS
2008 New Delhi

SHORT INTRODUCTION TO VAISNAVISM

First published by COSMO 2008

ISBN 978-81-307-0908-6

Published by
COSMO PUBLICATIONS
for
GENESIS PUBLISHING PVT. LTD.
24-B, Ansari Road, Darya Ganj,
New Delhi-110 002,
INDIA

Printed in India by
Cosmo Publications

one

VAISHNAVISM: GENERAL CHARACTERISTICS, FOUR SECTS

The Hindūs of the present day may be broadly divided into three principal classes[1], namely, (1) Smārtas, (2) Śaivas, (3) Vaishṇavas.

The first class believe that man's spirit is identical with the one infinite Spirit (Ātmā, Brahmā[2]), which is the substratum of the Universe and only cognizable through internal meditation and self-communion. They regard that Spirit as the highest object of all religious knowledge and aspiration. They are also belivers in the Tri-mūrti; that is, in the three personal gods, Brahmā, Vishṇu, and Siva—with their train of subordinate deities—but only as coequal manifestations of the one eternal impersonal Spirit, and as destined ultimately to be reabsorbed into that Spirit and so disappear. This, I repeat, is the only orthodox form of Brāhmincal religious thought, and those who follow it claim Śaṅkara as their chief leader and authoritative guide. It is a form of Pantheism, but differs widely from that of European philosophical systems.

The second great religious class of the Hindūs consists of the Śaivas, who, as we have seen, are believers in one god Śiva, not only as the Dissolver and Regenenator, but as the one supreme personal God, the one self-existent Being, identified with the one Spirit of the universe, and therefore not liable to lose his personality by reabsorption into that

Spirit.

The third class consists of the Vāishṇavas, who are believers in the one personal god Vishṇu, not only as the Preserver, but as above every other god, including Śiva. It should be noted, too, that both Śaivas and Vāishṇavas agree in attributing an essential form and qualities to the Supreme Being. Their one God, in fact, exists in an eternal body, which is antecedent to his earthly incarnations and survives all such incarnations.

Vaishṇavism then is, like Śaivism, a form of Monotheism. It is the seting aside of the triune equality of Brahmā, Śiva, and Vishṇu in favour of one god Vishṇu (often called Hari), especially as manifested in his two human incarnations Rāma and Krishṇa. 'Brahmā and Śiva,' said the great Vaishnava teacher Mādhva, 'decay with their decaying bodies; greater than these is the undecaying Hari.' And here, at the outset of an important part of our subject, I must declare my belief that Vāishṇavism, notwithstanding the gross polytheistic superstitions and idolatry to which it gives rise, is the only real religion of the Hindū peoples, and has more comon ground with Christanity than any other form of non-Christain faith. Vedism was little more than reverential awe of the forces of Nature and a desire to propitiate them. Brāhmanism was simply an Indian variety of pantheistic philosopy. Buddhism, which was a product of Brāhmanism, gained many followers by its disregard of caste distinctions and its offers of deliverance from the fires of passion and miseries of life; but, in its negations and denials of the existence of both a Supreme and human spirit, was no religion at all; and in this respect never commended itself generally to the Indian mind. Śaivism, though, like Vānishṇavism, it recognized the eternal personality of one Supreme Being, was too severe and call a system to exert exclusive influence over the great majority of the Hindu populations. Vāishṇavism alone possesses the essential elements of a genuine religion. For there can be no true religion without personal devotion to a personal God—without trusting Him, without loving Him, without praying to Him, and indeed without obeying Him.

Who can doubt that a God of such a character was needed for India,—a God who could satisfy the yearnings of the heart for a religion of faith, love and prayer rather than of knowledge and works? Such a God was believed to be represented by Vishṇu—the God who evinced his sympathy with mundane suffering, his interest in human affairs, and his activity for the welfare of all created things by frequent descents (avatāra) on earth, not only in the form of men, but also in non-and semi-human farms.

Hence, teachers arose (among whom was Śāṇḍilya the author of the Bhakti-sūtras) who insisted on the doctrine of salvation by faith (Bhaktī)—a doctrine dimly adumrated in portions of the Veda, and fully propounded in the Bhāgavad Gītā and Bhāgavata-purāṇa.

Intense faith, then, in a personal god is the chief characteristic of Vāishṇavism. Of course, it is merely the intensity of this faith that distinguishes the worship of Viṣhṇu from that of Śiva; for both Vaishṇavism and Śaivism agree in dissenting from the vague impersonal Pantheism of Brāhmincal philosophy, whose one God is the substratum of everything and himself nothing. Nor can we wonder that devotion to Vishṇu in his two human incarnations, Rāma and Krishṅa, became the most popular religion of India. These two heroes were of kingly Kshatrīya caste, and greatly beloved as popular leaders. It is usual to assert that the Brāhmans are the highest objects of worship and honour among the Hindūs. This is not the case among the countless adherents of the Vāishṇava religion. The mass of the people of India exalt the divine right of kings and the divine right of the government of the day above all other forms of power, and worship every great a heroic leader as an incarnation of the deity.

Yet, with all its popularity, Vaishṇavism is not an example of a house at peace within itself. It has spilt up into various subdivisons, which display no little of the odium theologicum in their opposition to each other. Possibly antagonism of some kind is a necessary condition of religious vitality. At any rate in India all religius systems inevitably break up into sects, and seem to gather strength and vigour from the process.

It is not uncommon, indeed, to hear it asserted that Hindūism is rapidly falling to destined soon to collapse altogether. One reason given for the doom supposed to be impending over its future is, that it is not a proselyting religion. And the truth certainly is that no stranger can be admitted as a convert to Hindūism either by making any particular confession of faith or by going through any prescribed forms. The only acknowledged mode of admission is by birth. To become a Hindū one must be born a Hindū. Yet Hindūism is continually growing within itself. In its tenacity of life and power of expansion it may be compared to the sacred banian-tree, whose thousand ramifications, often issuing from apparently lifeless stems, find their way into walls, undermine old buildings, or themselves descend to the ground, take root in the soil, and form fresh centres of growth and vitality.

And it cannot be doubted that one great conservative element of Hindūism is the many-sidedness of Vāishṇavism. For Vāishṇavism is, like Buddhism, the most tolerant of systems. It is always ready to accommodate itself to other creeds, and delights in appropriating to itself the religious ideas of all the nations of the world. It admits of every form of internal development. It has not organized hierarchy under one supreme head, but it may have any number of separate association under separate leaders, who are ever, banding themselves together for the extension of spiritual supermacy over ever-increasing masses of the population. It has no formal confession of faith, but it has an elastic creed capable of adaptation to all varieties of opinion and practice. It has no one Bible—no one collection of writings in one compact volume, like the Holy Bible, with lines of teaching converging towards one great central truth—but it has a series of sacred books, called Purāṇas, each of the which professes to be a direct revelation from the Supreme Being, and each of which may be used as an authority for the establishment of almost any kind of doctrine. It can, like Brāhmanism, be pantheistic, monotheistic, dualistic, polytheistic. It can, like Śaivism, enjoin asceticism, self-mortification, and austerity. It can, like Buddhism, preach liberty, equality, fraternity; or inculcate universal benevolence, and avoidance of injury to others. It can even set its face against idolatry[3], and can look with sympathizing condescension on other beliefs, or hold it to be a development of its own theory of religion suited to Europeans. It is owing to the all-comprehensivness of the Vāishṇava system that any new doctrine or any new view of old doctrine may be promulgated by any man of originality and ability, with an almost certain prospect of success. And indeed the religious credulity of the inhabitants of India increases in proportion to their unbelief in all political and social innovations. Broken up as they are into a multitude of separate peoples, few in this country have any desire for national union or intellectual progress. Few wish to leave the path troden by their forefathers, or deviate from the old traditions. The masses of the various populations can neither read nor write. They care nothing for science. History, biography, and political economy are to them a terra incognita. Their whole desire is to be left undistrubed in their time-honoured customs, family traditions, and caste usage.

One only subject has power to rouse them from their normal condition of mental torpor. That subject is Religion (in close connection with caste) is ever present to a Hindū's mind. It colours all his ideas. It runs through every fibre of his being. It is the very Alpha and Omega of his whole earthly career. He is born religious, and dies religious. He is religious in his eating and drinking, in his sleeping and waking, in his dressing and undressing, in his rising up and sitting down, in his work and amusement. Nay, religion attends him in antental ceremonies long before his birth, and follows him in endless offerings for the good of his soul long after death. Let any one appear as an earnest preacher of religion in any assemblage of ordinary Hindūs—let him announce that he has come as a messenger from heaven, or even that he is prepared to work mircales in attestation of the truth of his mission, and he is sure of being believed. And if to his other qualifications he adds a character for self-denial and asceticism, he cannot fail to attract disciples; for nowhere in the world are family ties so binding as in India, and yet nowhere is such homage paid to their abandonment. The influence of any new religious leader (ācārya) who is known to live a life of abstinence, bodily mortification, and suppression of the passions, is sure to become unbounded, either for good or evil.

Probably, during the leader's lifetime, he is able to restrain the enthusiasm of his converts within reasonable limits. It is only when he dies that they are apt to push his opinions to extremes never intended by himself. Eventually they develop his teaching into an overgrown unhealthy system, not appreciated disgusts all sensible men, even among its own adherents. Then some new teacher arises to re-establish purity of doctrine. He is, of course, in his turn a man of earnestness and energy, with a strong will, and great powers of persuasion. He collects around him with equal facility a number of followers, and those in their turn carry his teaching to great lengths.

Hence the condition of Vāishṇavism, which depends far more than Śaivism on personal leadership and influence, is one of perpetual decay and revival, collapse and recovery. Its fluctuations resemble those of a vast ocean heaving this way and that in continual flux and reflux.

It is doubtless true that all human systems are liable to similar alternations. But in India every tendency of humanity seems intensified and exaggerated. No country in the world is so conservative in its traditions. Yet no conutry has undergone so many religious changes and vicissitudes. To follow out in detail the whole drama of Vāishṇavism would require volumes. Even the first act presents us with a succession of shifting scenes.

In all likelihood the primary idea of a god Vishṇu (a name derived from root *vish*, 'to pervade'), permeating and infusing his essence into material objects, was originally connected with the personification of the infinite heavenly space. We know that in the Rig-veda Vishṇu is a form of the ever-moving solar orb, and in a well-known hymn (I, 22, 16, 17), still commonly used by the Brāhmans, he is described as astriding through the seven worlds[4] in three steps, and enveloping the universe with the dust of his beams. A later work, the Aitareya-brāhmaṇa of the Ṛig-veda, opens with the following remarkable statement: 'Fire (Agnī) has the lowest place among the gods, Vishṇu the highest; between them stand all the other deities.' (Haug's edition, 1.)

Elsewhere the god Vishṇu is connected with water. In Manu's Law-book (I. 10) the Suprteme Spirit is called Nārāyaṇa, as moving on the waters; in harmony with which idea Vishṇu is often represented in sculptures, images, and pictures as Nārāyaṇa in human form, reposing on the thousand-headed serpent and floating on the ocean.

In the later mythology of Brāhmanism, when the doctrine of the traid of personal gods (Tri-mūrti) had been fully developed and Vishṇu had taken his place as the second person of that traid, he has a less distinctly marked human personality, antecedent to his incarnations, than the god Śiva.

To write a biographical account of the god Vishṇu's life in his own heavenly abode, like the life of his rival Śiva, would be difficult. The truth is that the development of his human personality, which is really greater than that of any other gods in the Hindū pantheon, must be looked for on earth in the forms of Rāma and Krishṇa.

Nevertheless in his antecedent condition as Vishṇu, this deity has a material character and individuality of his own quite irrespective of his incarnations. He is described as living in Vaikuṅtha—a locality, as we have seen, more inaccessible and less easy to identify with any definite spot on earth than Śiva's abode Kailāsa. He has a wife Lakshmī or Śrī, the goddess of fortune and beauty, who is fabled to have sprung, with other precious things, from the froth of the ocean when churned by the gods and demons. And as Vishṇu in his non-Avātāra condition lives a life which has fewer features in common with humanity than that of Śiva, so is his wife Lakshmī less human than Śiva's wife Pārvatī. In fact the more human side of both the god and goddess is reserved for their descents in human form—Vishṇu as Rāma and Krishṇa, Lakshmī as Śītā and Rādhā. Nevertheless some details of Vishṇu's separate personality as distinct from his Avatāras may be gathered from the purāṇas. For example, we are told that he has a peculiar auspicious mark (Śrī-vatsa) on his breast[5]. He has four arms, and holds a symbol in each of his four hands; namely, a wheel or circular weapon (Cakra) called SudarŚana, a conch-shell[6] (Śaṅkha) called Pāñcjanya, a club (gadā) called Kaumodakī, and a lotus-flower (padma). Buddhism in all probability borrowed this circular symbol which was originally significant the wheel of the Buddhistic law, or of the cosmical cycles peculiar to that system. Or, bearing in mind Vishṇu's connection with the Sun, we may reasonably regard it as emblematical of the Sun's circular course in the heavens[7]. In the later mythology it is supposed to represent a missile weapon hurled by Vishṇu, like a quoit, at the demons who are ever plotting evil against gods and men, and with whom he is always at war[8]. Similarly the conch-shell is blown by him like a trumpet in his battles; its miraculous sound filling his enemies with terror and helping him to secure victory. The club is also used in Vishṇu's conflict with his demon-foes. Moreover he is armed with a wonderful bow called Śārṅga and a sword Nāndaka. He has a jewel on his wrist named Syamantaka, and another on his breast called Kaustubha. When he has occasion to move through space he is borne on the mythical bird Garuda[9], closely related to the Sun and comapred to an eagle, but represented as semi-human in form and character, with a bird-like face. Possibly this Garuda may be a personification of the sky or ethereal element which supports Vishṇu—identified with the Sun—one of whose names is 'Air-borne' (vāyu-vāhana). It is noteworthy that Garuda, like the Kṛishṇa form of Vishṇu, is the destroyer of serpents which typify sin and evil. Yet serpents have also their contrary character, and even divine attributes; for at the dissolution of the Universe and between the intervals of creation, Vishṇu, as the Supreme Being, reclines in profound repose on the thousand-headed serpent Śesha—typical of infinity—while his wife Lakshmī chafes his feet, and out of his navel grows the lotus which supports Brāhmā, the active agent in reproducing the world. Finally, Vishṇu has the river Ganges issuing from one of his feet, whence it flows through the sky before it falls on the head of the god Śiva.

And here it may be noted that the devotional enthusiasm of Vishṇu's worshippers has endowed him with a thausand names and epithets.[10] This is exactely eight less than the Śaivas have lavished on Śiva, and, considering the rivalry between the followers of the two deities, must be regarded as a modest allowance. The repetition of any or all of these names (nāma-saṇkīrtana), either with or without the help of a rosary, constitutes an important part of daily worship, and is effective of vast stores of religious merit. They are all enumerated with those of Śiva in the Anuśāsaṅa-parva of the Mahābhārata.[11]

In comparing the two catalogues it is intersting to observe

how many names are common to both deities. Vishṇu, especially, has a large number of names which he shares with the rival god, and is even called Śiva 'the Auspicious;' while Śiva is called Vishṇu, the Pervader, each in fact deities is allotted an ample assortment of the usual titles expressive of almighty power-such as all-creating, all-seeing, all-knowing, infinite, self-existent, all-pervading-mixed up with many which are necessarily claiming divine homage. Vishṇu has certainly fewer objectionable ephithets than Śiva.

Many names of both gods are simply taken from those of the Sun, Fire, and wind; and many are expressive of lofty divine attributes—once believed to be the peculiar property of Christian theology. For example, Vishṇu is called 'the holy Being' (*Pavitram*, also applied to Śiva), 'the True (Sātyaḥ), 'the Pure Spirit' (or 'having a pure spirit, 'Pūtātmā), 'the Way '(Mārgaḥ),' the Truth '(Tattvam), 'the Life' (Prāṇah), 'the Physician' (Vaidyaḥ), 'the World's Medicine' (Aushadham or Bheshajam Jagatah), 'the Father' (Pitā), and even 'the Holy of the Holy' (Pavitrm Pavitrāṇām)[12]—an epithet which it is not difficult to reconcile with some of the actions of his Kṛishṇa manifestation.

On the other hand, Śiva is called by the following names in addition to those already mentioned:—the Mother (Mātā, as well as Pitā, the Father), Extinction (Nirvāṇam), the Year-causer (Saṃvatsara-karah), the great Illusionist (Mahāmāyah), the Night-walker (Niuṣācarah), the Hidden File (Baḍavā-mukhah, 'Mare-faced'), the White One (Śuklah), the Enraged (Mahākrodhaḥ), the Root (Mūlam), the Ill-formed (Virūpaḥ), the Mule (Haya-gardabhiḥ, mixture of the questions of horse and ass?)

Again, some of Vishṇu's designations as Kṛishṇa, such as Pārtha-sārathi, 'Charioteer of Arjuna' (under which title he is worshipped at Madras), and VeṅkaṭeŚa, 'Lord of the hill Veṅkaṭa,' are, like those of Śiva, merely local epithets; and some (as for example Vithobā, worshiped at Pandharpur) are the restult of his identification with particular local heroes.

I need sparcely repeat that the chief distinguishing characteristic of the god Vishṇu is his condescending to infuse his essence into animals and men with the object of delivering his worshippers from certain special dangers or otherwise benefiting mankind. The peculiar nature of these so-called incarnations or descents (Āvatāra), and the vast difference between the Hindu and Christian idea of incarnation, have been already described. In some of the Purāṇas Vishṇu's incarnations are multiplied to the number of twenty-two, twenty-four, or even twenty-eight. But the ten which follow are those most generally known and believed in throughout India:—

1. **The Fish (Matsya).** Vishṇu is believed to have infused a portion of his essence into the body of a fish to save Manu[13], the primeval man and progentior of the human race, from the universal deluge. This Manu, like Noah, conciliated the Deity's favour by his piety and austerities in an age of universal depravity. Hence he was miraculously warned of the appraoching deluge, and was commanded to build a ship and go on board with the seven Rishis, or partiarchs, and the seeds of all existing things. Manu did so. The flood came, and Vishṇu took the form of a vast fish with a horn on its head, to which the ship's cable was fastened. The ship was thus supernaturally drawn along and secured to a high crag till the flood had passed.

2. **The Tortoise (Kūrma).** Vishṇu infused a portion of his essence into the body of an immense tortoise to aid in producing or recovering certain valuable articles, some of which had been lost in the deluge. For this purpose he stationed himself at the bottom of the sea of milk—one of the seven concentric circular seas surrounding the seven concentic circular continents of the earth—that his back might serve as a pivot for the mountain Mandara, around which the gods and demons twisted the great serpent Vāsuki. They then stood opposite to each othre, and using the snake

as a rope and the mountain as a churning-rod, churned the milky ocean violently till, one by one, fourteen inestimably valuable or typical objects emerged[14]. 1. The nectar confering imortatlity (Amrita). 2. The physician of the gods and holder of the nectar (Dhāṅvantari). 3. The goddess of good fortune and beauty, wife of Vishṇu (Lakshmī or Śrī). 4. The goddess of wine (Surā)[15]. 5. The moon (çandra). 6. The nymph Rambhā, celebrated as a kind of prototype of lovely women. 7. A fabulous high-eared horse (Uccaih-Śravas), the supposed prototype of the equine race. 8. The miraculous jewel Kaustubha, afterwards appropriated by Kṛishṇa. 9. A celestial tree (Pārijāta) yielding all desired objects. 10. The cow of plenty (Kāma-dhenu or Surābhi), granting all boons. 11. A mythical elephant (Airāvata)—afterwards appropriated by the god Indra—prototype of the elephantine race. 12. A sacred conch-shell (Śaṇkha), afterwards the property of Vishṇu (or Krishṇa), and supposed, when blown as a horn, to insure victory over his enemies (see note). 13. A miraculuous unerring bow (Dhānus).[16] 14. A deadly poision (Visha).

3. **The Boar (Varāha).** Vishṇu infused a portion of his essence into the body of a huge boar—symbolical of strength —to deliver the world from the power of the demon Hiraṇyāksha, who had seized the earth and carried it down into the depths of the ocean. The divine boar dived down into the abyss, and after a contest of a thousand years, slew the monster and brought back the earth to the surface. Another legend represents the earth as completely submerged by the deluge, and likely to remain for ever lost in the waters, had not the boar descended into the flood and with his mighty tusks upheaved it from its watery grave and made it fit to be reinhabited.

4. **The man-lion (Nara-siṇha).** Vishṇu assumed the shape of a creature half man, half lion, to deliver the world from the tyrant Hiraṇya-kaśipu, who had obtained a boon from Brahṃā that he should not be slain by either god or man or animal. Hence he became powerful enough to unsurp

the dominion of the three worlds. He even appropriated the sacrifices intended for the gods and necessary for their support. When his pious son Prahlāda praised Vishṇu, the tyrant tried to destroy the boy; but Vishṇu appeared suddenly out of the centre of a pillar in a shape neither god, man, nor animal, and tore Hiranya-kaśipu to pieces.

These first four incarnations are said to have taken place in the first and the best (satya) of the four ages of the world.

5. **The Dwarf (Vāmana).** In the second (Tretā) age of the world[17], Vishṇu infused a portion of his essence into the body of a dwarf to wrest from the tyrant-demon Bali (the analogue of Rāvaṇa and Kaṇsa the two opponents of the Rāma and Kṛishṇa incarnations respectively) the dominion of the three worlds. The apparently contemptible little dwarf presented himself one day before the Tyrant, and solicited as much land as he could step in three paces. No sooner was his request granted than his form expanded, and he strode in two steps over heaven and earth, but out of compassion left the lower world in the demon's possession.

6. **Rāma with the axe (Paraśu-rāma).** Vishṇu infused a portion of his essence into the axe-armed Rāma, son of the Brāhman Jamadagni and descendent of Bhṛigu, in the second age, to prevent the military caste, or Kshatriyas, from tyran-nizing over the Brāhmanical. Paraśu-rāma is said to have cleared the earth twenty-one times of the whole Kshatriya race.

7. In the seventh descent Vishṇu infused half of his essence into the great hero **Rāma**, commonly called Rāma-candra, 'the beautiful or moon-like Rāma.'[18] This celebrated hero, who afterwards became an object of worship throughout a great part of India, was believed to have been manifested as an incarnation of Vishṇu at the close of the second or Tretā age to destroy the tyrant—demon Rāvaṇa who regined in Ceylon. India was never under one monarch, and in

ancient times its kings were simply petty princes and chieftains, who ruled over districts of more or less extended area, and Oudh (Ayodhyā) was probably one of the more powerful principalities. As a historical fact Rāma was no doubt one of the four sons of a king of Oudh, named Daśaratha, of the so-called Solar race, and therefore a Kshatriya. He is celebrated throughout India as the model son, brother, and husband, who was banished by his father to the Southern forests. There his pattern-wife Sitā was carried off by Rāvaṇa, the tyrant-king of Ceylon, and recovered by Rāma after making a bridge of rocks to the island. He was aided by Hanumān—a powerful chief of one of the aboriginal tribes, poetically compared to monkeys. This story forms the subject of one of the two great Indian Epics—the Rāmayaṇa—and no story in the world has obtained a wider circulation and celebrity. Every man, woman, and child in India is familiar with Rāma's exploits for the recovery of his wife, insomuch that a common phrase for an ignorant person is 'one who does not know that Sitā was Rāma's wife.' From Kaśmīr to Cape Comorin the name of Rāma is on every one's lips. All sects revere it, and show their reverence by employing it on all occasions. For example, when friends meet it is common for them to salute each other by uttering Rāma's name twice (Rāma-Rāma). Then no name is more commonly invoked in the hour of death. It is a link of union for all classes, castes, and creeds. And yet it is highly probable that during his lifetime Rāma received little more than the usual homage offered to every great, good, and brave man. His apotheosis did not take place till after his death, when he was converted into one of the most popular incarnations of Vishṇu; his ally Hanumān also receiving divine honours.

8. The eight descent was as **Kṛishṇa**, the dark hero-god; the most popular of all the later deities of India. This descent of Vishṇu at the end of the Dvāpara, or third age of the world, as the eighth son of Vasudeva and Devakī, of the Lunar race (Chandra-Vaṁsa) of chiefs, was for the

destruction of the tyrant Kaṇsa, the representative of the principle of evil—the analogue of Rāvaṇa in the previous incarnation.

According to some Kṛishṇa ought not to be reckoned as one of the ten Avatāras or descents of portion of Vishṇu's essence; for he was nothing short of Vishṇu's 'whole essence.' Those who hold this doctrine substitute Bala-rāma, 'the strong Rāma,' an elder son of Vasudeva and Devakī, and therefore elder brother of Kṛishṇa, as the eighth incarnation of Vishṇu. This Bala-rāma is more usually regarded as an incarnation of the great serpent Śesha. He is sometimes called the Indian Hercules, and for good reason. Many wonderful feats of strength are recorded of him, and he wields a formidable weapon in the shape of a plough-share, as well as a pestel-shaped club (musala). He is chiefly remarkable for his love of wine and strong drink, in which, along with his wife Revatī, he frequently indulges to the verse of inebriation.

The details of the later life of Kṛishṇa are interwoven with the later porions of the Mahābhārata, but do not belong to the plot, and might be omitted without impairing its unity. He is certainly not the hero of the great. He merely appears as a powerful chief[19] who takes the side of the real heroes-the Pāṇḍavas—and his claims to divine rank are often disputed during the progress of the story. Ever since his apotheosis Kṛishṇa although of the kingly caste he was brought up among cowherds, cowherdesses, and the families of peasants. His juvenile biography is given with much minuteness of detail in the Bhāgavata-purāṇa, from which we learn that Vāsudeva of the so-called Lunar race of princess—who probably occupied the part of India now called Rājputāna[20] had two wives, Rohiṇī and Devakī. The latter had eight sons, of whom the eighth was Kṛishṇa. It was predicted that one of the eight would kill Kaṇsa, chief of Mathurā, and cousin of Devakī. Kaṇsa therefore imprisoned Vasudeva and his wife, and slew their first six children. Bala-rāma, the seventh, was abstracted from Devakī's womb, transferred to that of Rohinī, and so saved. The eighth was Kṛishṇa, born with a black skin, and the mark Śrī-vatsa on his breast[21]. His father Vasudeva escaped from Mathurā with the child, and, favoured by the gods, found a certain herdsman named Nanda, whose wife had lately a child. To his care he consigned the infant Kṛishṇa. Nanda settled first in Gokula or Vraja, and afterwards in Vṛindāvana, where Kṛishṇa and Balarāma grew up together, roaming in the woods, and joining in the sports of the herdsman's sons and daughters. While still a boy, Kṛishṇa gave proof of his divine origin by working a few startling miracles. Thus he destroyed the serpent Kāliya—regarded as a type of sin and evil—by trampling and dancing on his head. He lifted up the mountain-range Govardhana on his finger to shelter the herdsmen's wives from the wrath of Indra. Yet in spite of these and other evidences of his supramundane nature and powers, Kṛishṇa is described as addicted to very mundane practices. He constantly sported with the Gopis or wives and daughters of the cowherd, of whom eight were his favourites, especially Rādhā. On attaining mature age Kṛishṇa migrater to Gujarāt, built Dvārikā on the coast of that country, and thither transported the inhabitants of Mathurā after killing Kaṇsa. Kṛishṇa is said to have had countless wives, and at least 108,000 sons, but they are purely mythical. Not one of them receives worship, unless it be Pradyumna, the reputed son of Kṛishṇa by Rukminī, and usually held to be an incarnation of Kāmadeva the god of love.

9. **Buddha.** The adoption of Buddha as one of the ten incarnations of Vishṇu appears to have been the result of a wise compromise with Buddhism; the Brāhmans asserting that Vishṇu in his compassion for animals descended on Vedic sceptical Buddha that he might bring discredit on Vedic sacrifices (see Gīta-govinda, I. 13); or, according to another theory, that wicked men might bring destruction on themselves by acepting Buddhism and denying the existence of the gods.

10. **Kalki or Kalkin.** The descent of Vishṇu in this character has not yet taken place. Nor is he to appear till the close of the fourth or Kali age, when the world has becomer wholly depraved. He is then to be revealed in the sky, seated on a white horse, with a drawn sword blazing like a comet, for the final destruction of the wicked, for the redemption of the good, for the renovation of all creations, and the restoration of the age of purity (Satya-yuga). From the fact of the horse playing an important role in this incarnation, it is sometimes called Aśvāvatāra. Indeed it is a remarkable fact that a belief in a coming Redeemer seems to exist in all religions, not exepting Buddhism and Muhammadanism[22].

Looking more closely at these ten special incarnations, we may observe that the god Vishṇu, in conformity with his character of a universal 'Pervader,' discharges his functions in his first three descents by pervading the bodies of animals. It is remarkable, too, that these three zoomorphic incarnations all have reference to the tradition of a general deluge. In his fourth descent Vishṇu takes the form of a being half animal, half man. Possibly this combinatin may be intended as a kind of intermediate link, to connect the deity with higher forms. From half a man, the transition is to a complete man, but the divine essence on passing into human forms commences with a dwarf—the smallest type of humanity. Thence it advances to mighty heores, sent into the world to deliver mankind from the oppression of tyrants—represented as evil demons—whose power increases with the increase of corruption and depravity during the four ages. The eighth is the highest and so to speak culminating incarnation; for Kṛishṇa is believed to be not a part of Vishṇu's essence, but a complete manifestation of Vishṇu himself. The ninth may be passed over as a mere device on the part of the Brāhmaṇs to account for the existence of Buddhism. The tenth and final incarnation, which remains to be revealed, will surpass all the others in importance. In it evil and wickedness are to be entirely rooted out, and the age of purity resorted. We may see in this connected series of what to us appear exceedingly of the Hindū idea of metempsychosis. Just as the souls of men, regarded as emanations from the Deity, pass into stones, plants, and animals, or rise to the bodies of higher beings, so portions of the essence of Vishṇu pass through regular stages of embodied existence of the maintenance of the order of the universe.

As we have already seen, Vishṇu's essence divided itself into male and female, but he had no childrrn in his Non-avatāra condition, as Śiva had, unless Kāma-deva, god of love, said to have been his mind-born son (afterwards incarnate in Pradyuman), be so regarded. When the male essence descended as Rāma, the female was born as Rāma's faithful wife Sītā; and when the male descended as Kṛishṇa, the female became Kṛishṇa's favourite Rādhā.

We now proceed to give a description of the more important Vaishṇava sects,—beginning, with those founded by Rāmānuja, Madhva, Vallabha, and Caitanya; and first we may direct attention to some points in which they all agree.

In the first place, it must be understood that all the sects agree in maintaining, at least theoretically, that devotion to Vishṇu supersedes all distinctions of caste. As a matter of fact, however, it is not to be supposed that a Vaishṇava Brāhman ever really gives up his claim to superiority over the inferior classes.

Next, it must be borne in mind that all the Vaishṇava sects are more or less opposed to the pure non-duality (advaita) of Śaṅkarācārya which makes the spirit of man identical with the one Spirit of the Universe (Ātmā, Brahmā).

Further, we may take note of the fact that the sacred book of all worshippers of Vishṇu in his most popular manifestation—that of the hero Kṛishṇa, with his favourite Rādhā—consists of two chief books, the Bhāgavata-purāṇa and the Bhagavad-gītā; and that those who pay exclusive adoration to the other popular manifestation of Vishṇu—the hero Rāma-also acknowlwdge two special sacred books in Vālmī's Rāmāyaṇa and in the Rāmāyaṇa of Tulsīdās. Undoubtedly these four books bought to find a prominent place among the 'Sacred Books' of India.

Then it must not be forgotten that all agree in the worship of existing religious teachers who are supposed to be embodiments, not only of divine wisdom, but of the very essence of divinity. In the foremost rank must always come the original founder of each particular sect, whose title is Ācārya. He is regarded as little inferior to Kṛishṇa himself, and may even be identified with him. As to the living teacher of the day, is not elevated to equal rank, he is a greater reality. He receives homage as a visible and tangible mediator between earth and heaven. He is to the mass of Vaishṇavas even more than a mediator between themselves and God. He is the living embodiment of the entire essence of the deity (sārva-deva-māyah). Nay, he is still more. He is the present god whose anger is to be deprecated and favour conciliated, because they make themselves instantly felt.

Next, all the Vāishṇava sects agree, as we have seen, in requiring a special ceremony of initiation (dīkshā) into their communion, accompanied by the repetition of a mantra (formula of words), significant of reverence for either Kṛishṇa or Rāma, such as, 'Reverence to great Kṛishṇah' (Śrī Krishṇa namaḥ), or eight-syallabled formula, 'Great Kṛishṇa is my refuge' (Śrī Kṛishṇah Śaraṇam nama).

Childern are admitted to the religion of Vishṇu at the age of three or four years. A rosary or necklace (kaṇthī) of one hundred and eight beads[23], usually made of tulsī wood, is passed round their necks by the officiating priest (Guru), and they are taught the use of one of the foregoing mantras, which is repeated by the Guru, very much as the sacred words 'In nomine Patris,' etc. are repeated by the priest at the Christian rite of baptism.

Then, at the age of twelve or thirteen, another rite is performed, corresponding to our confirmation. With the Vallabha sect it is called the 'Dedication rite' (Samarpaṇa); that is, the concesration of body, soul, and substance (tan, man, dhan) to Kṛishṇa; the mantra taught being to the following effect:—'I here dedicate to the holy Kṛishṇa my dobily organs, my life, my inmost soul, and its faculties, with my wife, my house, my childern, with all the wealth I may acquired here or hereafter, and my own self. O Kṛishṇa, I am thy servant.' These ceremonies may, in the case of all but Brāhmans, take the place of the initiatory rite of orthodox Brāhmanism, performed by investiture with the sacred thread (to be afterwards described).

Another general characteristics of all the Vaishṇava sects is tenderness towards animal life. In this respect Vaishṇavism contrasts favourably with Śaivism. No life must be taken by a worshipper of Vishṇu, not even that of a minute insect, and not even for sacrifice to a deity (as, for example to Kālī), and lest of all must one's own life be taken. But if deaths occur, they must be accidental, as self-destruction is wholly opposed both to the letter and spirit of the Vaishṇava religion.

Then, of course, the several sects agree in enjoining the use of the perpendicular coloured marks on the forehead, called Urdhva-puṇḍra. They are supposed to denote the impress of either one to both the feet of Vishṇu, and to possess great efficacy in shielding from evil influences and delivering from sin. In addition to these frontal marks, most of the sects brand the breast and arms with the circular symbol and conch-shell of Vishṇu.

Finally, all the sects believe that every faithful and virtuous worshipper of Vishṇu is transported to his heaven, called Vaikunṭha, or to that of Kṛishṇa, called Goloka (instead of to the temporary Svarga or paradise of orthodox Brāhmanism), and that when once admitted there, he is not liable to be born again on earth. There, according to the merit of its works, he may enjoy any of the three conditions of bliss, Sālokya, Sāmīpya, or Sārūpya, already described. Whether a Viashṇava may be supposed capable of achieving the highest condition of beatification—conscious absorption into the divine essence (Sāyuja)—depends of course on the philosophical views of the sect to which he belongs. One point requires to be understood in comparing the Vaishṇava religion with Chirstianity—namely, that God with Hindū Theists, can only be propitiated by works. He may be called merciful, but He only shows mercy to those who deserve it by their actions, and if He accepts faith it is only because this also is a meritorious act. Every man's hope of heaven depends on his own self-righteousness and on the amount of merit he has been able to accumulate during life. We must also bear in mind that although Vishṇu is supposed to be a Creator as well as a Saviour, yet he is not so in the Christian sense of the word; for all sects believe in some material cause (upādana) some eternal substance out of which the Universe is formed.

Let us now advert to the principal points of difference between the more conspicuous Vaishṇava sects, beginning with that founded by the celebrated reformer, Rāmānuja.

Sect founded by Rāmānuja

Rāmānuja, or as he is often called Rāmānujācārya, was born about the twelfth century at Stri (Śrī) Parambattūr, a town about twenty-six miles west of Madras. He is known to have studied and taught at Kāñcīpuram (Conjīvaram), and to have resided towards the end of his life at Śrī-Rangam, on the river Kāverī, near Trinchinopoly, where for many years he wordshipped Vishṇu in his character of Srīraṅganāth. The distinctive point of his teaching according to the Sarva-darśana-saṅgraha (translated by Professors Cowell and Gough), was his assertion of the existence of a traid of principle (padārtha-tritayam), namely, 1. the Supreme Being (Iśvara); 2. soul (cit); and 3. non-soul (a-cit), Vishṇu is the Supreme Being; individual spirits are souls; the visible world (dṛiśyaṃ) is non-soul. All three principles have an eternal existence distinct from each other.

This doctrine ws clearly antagonistic to that of the great Brāhmanical revivalist Śānkara, who lived three on four centuries before. According, to Śānkara, as we have seen, the separate existence of the spirit of man, as distinct from the one Universal Spirit, was only illusory. Illusion (Māyā), too—existing from all eternity—was the only material or substantial cause (upādāna-kārana) of the external world, though this eternally creative Illusion was powerless to create the world exccpt in union with the one Spirit. Rāmānuja, on the other hand, contended that the souls or spirits of men are truly, essentially, and eternally distinct and different from the one Universal Spirit. With regard to the external world his views appear to have been less dualistic than those of the Sāṅkhya, and even than those of the Vedānta, for in the former we have Prakṛiti and in the latter Māyā, as the material cause (upādāna) out of which the Universe was created; whereas Rāmānuja held that God is himself both the creator (Kartā) of the world and the substantial cause or material out of which it is formed. He appears to, have asserted that the world and God stand towards each other in the relation of body and soul, and that body and soul are virtually one. It will be found, in fact, that the doctrine 'ex nihilo nihil fit' in some form or other holds good in every religious system which India has produced independently of Christian influences.

In support of the doctrine that the spirits of men are really and eternally distinct from the one Universal Spirit he appealed to a passage in the Muṇḍaka Upanishad, which rests on a well-known text of the Ṛig-vedā (I. 164-20): 'Two birds—the Supreme and Individual Souls—always united, of the same name, occupy the same tree (abide in the same body). One of them (the individual Soul) enjoys the fruit of the fig, (or consequence of acts), the other looks on as a witness.'

Nevertheless Rāmānuja admitted the dependence of the human soul on the divine, and urgeed the duty of striving after complete, though conscious-union with the Supreme-identified with Vishṇu:—'Cut is the knot of man's heart, solved are all his doubts, ended are all his works, when he has beheld the Supreme Being[24].'

A good account of Rāmānuja's opinions is given by Dr. K. M. Banerjea in his *Dialogues on Hindū Philosophy*. The account is founded on extracts taken from the writings of one of Rāmānuja's disciples, and from Rāmānuja's own work on the Vedānta-sūtras (called śārīraka-bhāshya).

We may suppose Rāmānuja himself to be speaking as follows:—

> 'All the Śāstras tell us of principles—knowledge and ignorance, virtue and vice, truth and falsehood. Thus we see pairs everywhere, and God and the human soul are also so. How can they be one? I am sometimes happy, sometimes miserable. He, the Spirit, is always happy. Such is the discrimination. How then can two distinct substances be identical? He is an eternal Light, without anything to obscure it—pure, the one superintendent of the world. But the human soul is not so. Thus a thunder-bolt falls on the tree of no-distinction. How canst thou, oh slow of thought, say, I am He, who has established this immense sphere of the universe in its fulness? Consider thine own capacities with a candid mind. By the mercy of the Most High a little understanding has been committed to thee. It is not for thee, therefore, O perverse one, to say, I am God. All the qualities of sovereignty and activity are eternally God's. He is therefore a Being endowed with qualities (saguṇa). How can He be devoid of Qualities (nirguṇa)? Why, again, should this useless illusion be exercised? If you say, as a sport—

why should a being of unbounded joy engage in sport? To say that God has projected an illusion for deluding His creatures, or that, being essentailly devoid of qualities under the influence of illusion (*māyā*), is equally opposed to godliness. You cannot, if you believe Him to be all turth, allow the possibility of His projecting a deceptive spectacle. Nor can you, if you believe Him to be all knowledge and all power, assent to the theory of His creating anything under the influence of avidyā, or ignorance.'

Yet, notwithstanding the manifestly dualistic teaching of Rāmānuja in regard to the Supreme and human soul, he is usually credited with a qualified acquiescence in the Advaita doctrine of Śaṇkara. According to some, in fact, he merely propounded a new view of the Vedānta non-duality (a-dvaita) doctrine, giving it that peculair interpretation which is usually called 'qualified non-duality' (viśishṭādvaita). I found that no adherent of the Rāmānuja system in India was able to explain this peculiar view satisfactorily. It is, however, supposed by a passage in the Sarva-darśana-saṅgraha, where it is stated Rāmānuja's teaching, regarded from different points of view was open to the charge of admitting the three ideas of unity, duality, and plurality. Unity, it alleges, was admitted by him in saying that all individual spirits and visible forms constitute the body of the one Suprme Spirit. Duality was admitted in saying that the spirit of God and man are distinct. Plurality was admitted in saying that the Spirit of man which is multitudinous, and the visible world are distinct. (Cowell and Gough's translation, pp. 73, 75.) The first of these admissions is said to amount to qualified unity, and is therefore styled Viśishṭādvaita.

Rāmānuja also held that at great periodical dissolutions of the Universe human souls and the world are re-absorbed into God, but without lossing their own separate identity. In the Tattva-muktāvali (tranṣlated in Dr. Banerjea's 9th Dialogue) we find Rāmānuja represented as saying, 'Many flavours of trees there are in honey, and they are separable from it.

How otherwise could it remove the three-fold disorders ? Souls, in like manner, are absored in the Lord at the dissolutions of all things, but are not unified with Him, for they are again separated at the creation. As there is difference between rivers and the sea, between sweet and salt waters, so is there a difference between God and Souls, because of their characteristic distinctions. Rivers when joined with the sea, are not altogether unified with it, though they appear inseparable. There is a real differnece betwen salt and sweet waters. Even milk, when mixed with milk, and water with water, do not obtain unification, merely because they are supposed to be unified. Neither do souls when absorbed in the Supreme Being, obtain identity with Him[25].'

With regard to the various manifestations of the Supreme Being and the duty of worshipping Him, Rāmānuja held that God is present among His votaries on earth in five ways: 1. in images; 2. in divine embodiments (such as Rāma); 3. in full manifestations (such as Kṛishṇa); 4. in the subtle (sūkshma) all-pervading spirit; 5. in the internal Spirit controlling the human soul (antaryāmin). The worshipper may be incapable of rising at once to any high act of adoration; in which case he must begin by adoring Vishṇu as manifested in the first of these five ways—that is to say, in images and idols. He may afterwards ascend by regualar steps through the other four modes of worship till he reaches the fifth. If he never succeeds in attaining to this highest stage and so becomes capable of worshipping the internal Spirit enshrined in his own heart, Vishṇu identified with that Spirit raises him to his own heaven Vaikuṇṭha, whence there is no return to human existence, and where he enjoys the exquisite bliss of conscious assimilation to the God whom he has adored on earth, and even of concious absorption into that God[26]. Possibly this theory of concious absorption may constitute another reason for attributing the doctrine called 'qualified non-duality' (viśishṭā-dvaita) to Rāmānuja. Nevertheless the impression left on the mind by the account of his system in the Sarva-darśana-saṅgraha is that Rāmānuja was even more opposed to the doctrine of unity in regard to the divine and human souls than his brother sectarian Madhva. This impression is borne out by the fact that his system is treated of before that of Mādhva, and so placed lower down in that ascending scale which is supposed to culminate in the orthodox Ādvaita. Probably the real reason for its being so placed is that he asserts three principles—the Spirit of God, the spirit of man, and the visible world as his first axiom, whereas Madhva only asserts two.

After Rāmānuja's death, his numerous followers corrupted his teaching in the usual manner, introducing doctrines and practices which the founder of the sect had not enjoined and would not have sanctioned. Then, about six hundred years ago, a learned Brāhman of Kānjīvaram, named Vedāntācārya, put himself forward as a reformer, giving out that he was commissioned by the god Vishṇu himself to purify the faith—to sweep away corrupt incrustations, and restore the doctrines of the original founder. These doctrines, he affirmed, had been more carefully preserved by the Northern Brāhmans than by those in the South. Hence arose irreconcilable differences of opinion, which resulted in two great antagonistic parties of Rāmānujas—one called the northern school, Veda-galai (for Vada-kalai, Sanskṛit kalā), the other the southern school, Ten-galai (for Ten-kalai[27]). They are far more opposed to each other than both the parties are to Śaivas. The southern have compiled a Veda of their own, called 'the four thousand verses' (Nālāyira), written in Tamil, and held to be older than the Sanskṛit Veda, but really based on its Upāṇishad portion. In all their worship they repeat selections from these Tamil verses.

An important difference of doctrine, caused by different views of the nature of the soul's dependence on Vishṇu, separates the two parties. The view taken by the Vāda-galais corresponds, in a manner, to the Arminian doctrine of 'free-will.' The soul, say they, lays hold of the Supreme

Being by its own will, act, and effort, just as the young monkey clings to its mother. This is called the monkey-theory (markata-nyāya). The view of the Ten-galais is a counterpart of that of the Calvinists. It is techanically styled 'the cat-hold theory' (mārjāra-nyāya). The human soul, they argue, remains passive and helpless until acted on by the Supreme Spirit, just as the kitten remains passive and helpless until seized and transported, nolens volens, from place to place by the mother-cat.

Again, the Ten-galais maintain that that the Śakti or wife of Vishṇu is a created and finite being, though divine, and that she acts as a mediator or minister (purusha-kāra), not as an equal channel of salvation; wheras the Vada-galais regard her as, like her consort, infinite, and uncreated, and equally to be worshipped as a channel or means (upāya) by which salvation may be attained. I heared it remarked by a learned Ten-galai Brāhman that no educated men believe Vishṇu to be really married. 'What most Ten-galais hold,' he said, 'is that Lakshmī is an ideal personfication of the deity's more feminine attributes, such as those of mercy, love, and compassion; while some philosophers contend that the Hindū Gods are only represented with wives to typify the mystical union of the two eternal principles, spirit and matter for the production of the Universe. The central red mark, therefore, is, in case, the mere expression of trust in God's mercy; in the other, of beliefs in the great mystery of creation and re-creation.

No Arminians and Calvinists have ever fought more rancorously over their attempts to solve insoluble difficulties then have Vada-galais and Ten-galais over their struggles to secure the ascendency of their own theological opinions. The fight has ended in a drawn battle. The two opposite parties, exhausted with their profitless logomachy and useless strivings after an impossible unity of opinion, have agreed to differ in abstruse points of doctrine.

Their disputes are now chiefly confined to externals of the most trivial kind. It is the old story repeated. The Sibboleths are intolerant of the Shibboleths. The Vada-galais contend that the frontal mark of the sect ought to represent the impress of the right foot of Vishṇu (the supposed source of the divine Ganges), while the Ten-galais maintain that equal reverence is due to both the God's feet. It is certainly convenient from a social point of view that a man's religious idiosyncrasies should be stamped upon his forehead. Accordingly, the two religious parties are most particular about their frontal emblems, the Vada-galais making a simple white line between the eyes, curved to represent the sole of one foot, with a central red mark emblematical of Lakshmī terminating at the bridge; while the Ten-galais employ a more complicated device symbolical of both feet, which are suppossed to rest on a lotus throne, denoted by a white line drawn half down the nose. The complete Ten-galai symbol has the appearance of a trident, the two outer prongs (painted with white earth) standing for Vishṇu's two feet, the middle (painted red or yellow) for his consort, Lakshmī, and the handle (or white line down the nose) representing the lotus throne. The worst quarrels between the two divisions of the sect arise from disputes as to which mark is to be impressed on the images worshipped in the Vāishṇava temples, to which all Rāmānujas resort in differently. Tedious and expansive law-suits were often the result.

Both sects, however, agree in stamping or branding the same emblems of Vishūu—the discuss, the conch-shell, the club, and the lotus, generally the former two—on their breasts and arms.

Another point which distinguishes the Ten-galais is that they prohibit their widows from shaving their heads. Every married woman in India rejoices in long, fine hair, which she is careful to preserve intact. In the case of men, regular shaving is not only a universal custom, it is a religious duty. But for women to be deprived of any portion of their hair is a shame. A short female head is throughout India the chief mark of widowhood. Every widow, though a mere child, is compelled to submit her growing locks periodically to the family barber. It is, therfore, a singular circum—stance-quite in India—that the Ten-galai widows are exempted from all obligation to dishonour their heads in this manner [28] (Compare i Cor. xi, 5.).

Again, a pecularity common to both Rāmānuja sects is the strict privacy with which they eat and even prepare their meals. No Indians like to be looked at while eating. They are firm believers in the evil influence of the human eye (drishtī-dosha). The preparation of food is with high-caste natives an affair of equal secrecy. The Europeans can scarcely understand the extent to which culinary operations may be associated with religion. The kitchen in every Indian household is a kind of sanctuary or holy ground; almost as hallowed as the room dedicated to the family Gods. No unprivileged person must dare to intrude within this sacred enclosure. The mere galance of a man of inferior caste makes the greatest delicacies uneatable, and if such a glance happens to fall on the family supplies during the cooking operations, when the ceremonial purity of the water used[29] is a matter of almost life or death to every member of the household, the whole repast has to be thrown away as if poisoned. The family is for that day dinnerless. Food thus contaminated would, if eaten, communicate a tiant to the souls as well as bodies of the eaters—a taint which could only be removed by long and painful expiation. In travelling over every part of India, and diligently striving to note the habits of the natives in every circumstances of their daily life, I never once saw a single Hindū, except of the lowest caste, either preparing or eating cooked food of any kind. The Rāmānujas carry these ideas to an extravagant extreme. They carefully lock the doors of their kitchens and protect their culinary and prandial operations from the gaze of even high-caste Brāhmans of tribes and sects different from their own.

Each of the present chiefs (ācāryas) of the two Rāmānuja sects lays claim to be the true descendant of the founder himself in regular, unbroken succession. The Vada-galai successor (named Ahobala) lives at a monastery (Māṭha) in the Kurnool district. The Ten-galai successor (named Vānamāmala) lives in the Tinnevelly district. Though they preside over monasteries, they are both married; whereas the successors of the orthodox Brāhman Śankara, who live at Śṛiṅgeri in Mysore, are always celibates. The two Rāmānuja Ācāryas, however, are strict Ayengār Brāhmans, and will probably in their old age become Sannyāsīs, according to the teaching of the ancient law giver Mānu, who obtained that the atainment of great nearness to the Supreme Being is incompatible with the discharge of household duties, and that every Brāhman as he advances in life is bound to give up all family ties.

Each Ācārya makes a periodical visitation of his divotees, and holds a kind of confirmation in every large town. That is to say, every child or young person who has been initiated is brought before him to be branded or stamped as a true follower of Vishṇu. Boys may be branded at the age of seven or upwards; girls only after their marriages. A sacred fire is kindled, two golden instruments are heated, and the symbols of the wheel-shaped discus and conch-shell of Vishṇu are impressed on the breast, arms, or other parts of the body. I was informed by an intelligent Brāhman at Madurā that the Ācārya or chief of the sect from the Ahobala Matha visits that town once every eight or ten years, when as many young persons as possible take the opportunity of being branded. Even those who have been invested with the Brāhmanical thread require the addition of the Vaishṇava brand. The Ācārya is put to no expense. He is the guest of some well-to-do Brāhman in the town, and reaps a rich harvest of fees.

We pass on to the second great Vaishṇava sect—that founded by Mādhva—whose adherents are called Mādhvās. They are chiefly found in Southern India.

Sect founded by Mādhva

The next most important of the Vaishṇavas sects is that of the Mādhvas. They were founded by a Kanarese Brāhman named Mādhva—otherwise called Ānanda-tīrtha—said to have been born about the year 1200 of our era, at a place called Udupī, on the western coast (sixty miles north of Mangalore), and to have been educated in a convent at Ananteśvar. His doctrine is commonly called Duality (Dvaita), and is well known for the intensity of its opposition to the non-duality (Advaita) doctrine of the great Vedāntist Śankarācārya. The school he founded is sometimes called Pūrṇa-Prajña—a name also applied to its founder.

In fact the teaching of Mādhva is by some thought to owe no little of its distinctive character to the influence of Christianity, which had made itself felt in the South India before the thirteenth century. No evidence whatever is forthcoming on this subject. Nor has his system really much common ground with Christianity. Nor would it be easy to give a throughly exhaustive acount of his doctrines[30]. Still their general drift may be correctly gathered from the Sārva-dārśana-saṅgraha, though the points in which he differs from Rāmānuja are rather obscurely stated in that work.

Of course, Mādhva, like Rāmānuja, taught that there was only one God, whose principle name was Vishṇu (or Harī), and who was the one eternal Supreme Being, all other Gods being subject to the law of universal periodical dissolution.

> 'Brahmā, Śiva, and the greatest of the gods decay with the decay of their bodies; greater than these is the undecaying Harī.' (Professor Gough's translation.)

Perhaps the chief distinctive feature of Mādhva's teaching

was that his first axiom asserted categorically that there are two separate eternal principles (instead of three, as asserted by Rāmānuja), and that these two are related as independent and dependent, as master and servant, as king and subject. The one is the independent principle, God (identified with Vishṇu), the other is the dependent principle consisting of the human soul, or rather souls, for they are innumerable.

It was Mādhva's unqualified denial of the unity of the Supreme and human spirits which made him the opponent of the followers of Śankara.

The Vedāntists maintained, as we have seen, that the difference between one thing and another and between one soul and another was wholly illusory and unreal. Mādhva affirmed that a real and inextinguishable duality was to be proved both by perception and by inference[31].

'The Supreme Lord,' said Mādhva, 'differs from the individual soul because he is the object of its obedience. A subject who obeys a king differs from that king. In their eager desire to be one with the Supreme Beings, the followers of Śaṅkara lay claim to the glory of his excellence. This is a mere mirage. A man with his tongue cut off might as well attempt to enjoy a large plantain.'

Again, according to Mādhva the Vedic text, 'This is Self—That art thou,' points to similarity, not identity.

> 'Like a bird and the string; like the juices of various trees; like rivers and the sea; like fresh and salt water; like a robber and the robbed; like a man and his energy; so are soul and the Lord diverse and for ever different.' (Translation.)

Nor have these two principles a qualified unity comparable to the union of soul and body, as affirmed by Rāmānuja. They are absolutely distinct. With regard to the visible world, he taught that its elements existed eternally in the Supreme Being, and were only creatd by Him in the sense of being shaped, ordered, and arranged by His power and will. Practically he seems to have asserted three principles quite as plainly as Rāmānuja did; for his doctrine was that when once the world had emanated from the Supreme essence it remained a distinct entity to all eternity. 'There is a difference,' he affirmed, 'between human souls and God, and a difference between the insentient world (jada) and God.' Probably he saw the difficulty of proving the existence of matter externally to the mind, and therefore contended himself with asserting two distinct principles. God it was not to be distinguished, as an original principle, from God, and was not even as distinct as soul and body, though when once produced it remained as distinct from its Producer as an effect from its cause[32].

According to Mādhva the Supreme being is to be honoured in three ways—by naming, by worship, and by branding.

The act of naming (nāma-karaṇa) is performed by giving a child one of the thousand names of vishṇu—such as Keśva—as a memorial of his dedication to the service of the god.

The act of worship is threefold:—(1) with the voice by veracity, right conversation, kind words, and repetition of the Veda; (2) with the body—by giving alms to the poor, by defending and protecting them; (3) with the heart—by mercy, love, faith. This is a mere repetition of the old triple divisions of duties, according to thought, word, and deed.

With regard to the rite of branding (called aṅkana), the Mādhva sect, like the Rāmānuja and other Vaishṇavas, lay great stress on making the body indelibly with the circular discuss and shell of Vishṇu. They firmly believe that it is the duty of Vaishṇavas to carry throughout life a memorial of their God on their persons, and that such a lasting outward and visible sign of his presence will help them to obtain salvation through him.

'On his right arm let the Brāhman wear the discuss, on his left the conch-shell !'

When I was at Tañjore I found that one of the successors of Mādhva had recently arrived on his branding-visitation. He was engaged throughout the entire day in stamping his disciples and receiving fees from all according to their means.

Texts are recited at the time of branding, and in Sāyaṇa-Mādhva's time the following prayer was said:—'O Discus (Sudarśana), brightly blazing, effulgent as ten million suns, show unto me, blind with ignorance, the everlasting way of Vishṇu. Thou, O Conch-shell, aforetime sprangest from the Sea, held in the hand of Vishṇu, adored by all the gods, to thee be adoration.' (*Sarva-darśana-saṇgraha*, Cowell and Gough, p. 92.)

I learnt, too, that no less than eight Ācāryas, each of whom is established with his disciples in different monasteries with temples attached, claim to be successors of Mādhva. There are, however, only two principle religious parties among the Mādhvas. No doubt these quarre lover their Shibboleths, but not, I believe, with as much bitterness as the two divisions of Rāmānujas.

The frontal mark of all the Mādhvas is the same, consisting of two thin vertical lines meeting below in a curve, like that of the Vada-galai Rāmānujas. But a central black line is generally made with charcoal taken from incense burnt before the idols of Vishṇu.

So much for the doctrines of two sects which are worthy of especial attention. Perhaps Mādhva's system is the more interesting in its relation to European thought, but is Theism, like that of Rāmānuja and of every other Hindū Theistic system, differed widely in many important points from the Theism of Chiristianty, especially in making God the substantial as well as efficient cause of the visible world.

Sect founded by Vāllabha

The third great Vaishṇava sect is that founded by Vāllabha, or as he is commonly called Vallabh Ācāya, said to have been born in the forest of Campāraṇya about the year 1479. He was believed to have been an embodiment of a portion of Kṛishṇa's essence, and various miraculous stories are fabled about him. For instance, his intelligence is alleged to have been so great that when he commenced his education to have years of age, he mastered the four Vedās, the six systems of Philosophy, and the eighteen Purāṇas in four months.

After precocity so prodigious he was able at the age of twelve to formulate a new view of the Vaishṇava creed, but one which was to be a certain extent derived from a previus teacher named Vishṇusvāmī. Soon he commenced travelling to propagate his doctrines. When he reached the court of Kṛishṇadeva, king of Vijayanagar, he was invited to engage in a public disputation with a number of Smārta Brāhmans. In this he succeded so well that he was elected chief Ācārya of the Vaishāavas. He then travelled for nine years through different parts of India, and finally settled in Benares, where he composed seventeen works, among which was a commentary on the Bhāgavata-purāna. This last work, especially its tenth book—descriptive of the early life of Krishṇa—is the chief authoritative source of the doctrines of the sect. Vallabhācārya's view of the Vaishṇava creed has been called Pushṭi-mārga, the way of eating, drinking, and enjoying oneself. But in real fact he simply discountenanced asceticism as a mode of commending man to God. He maintained that worship of the Deity need not be accompanied with fasting, self-mortification, and suppression of the passions, but that the natural appetites were intended to be gratified, and the good things of this world to be enjoyed.

In philosopy Vallabha's opinions appear to have a greater leaning towards pure Vedāntism[33]. He is known to have died at Banares; but according to his followers, was transported to heaven while performing his adulations in the Ganges.

His followers are numerous in Bombay, Gujarāt, and Central India, particularly among the merchants and traders called Baniyas and Bhātiyas. He left behind him eighty-four principal disciples, who disseminated his doctrines in various directions. But the real successor to his Gādī (gaddī) or chair was his second son, Viṭṭhalnāth, sometimes called Gosāinjī from his having settled at Gokul, Kṛishṇa's abode near Mathura. This Viṭṭhalnāth had seven sons, each of whom established a Gādī in different districts, especially in Bombay, Kutch, Kāṭhiāwār, and Mālwa. The influence of Vallabhācārya's successors became so great that they received the title Mahārāja, 'great king,' the name Gosāin (for Gosvāmin—lord of cows—an epithet of Kṛishṇa) being sometimes added.

As was naturally to be expected, his followers exaggerated his teachings, especially in regard to his non-ascetical ways of religion. They have been called 'the Epicureans of India.' Thier spiritual leaders, the Mahārājas, dress in the costliest raiment, feed on the daintiest viands, and abandon themselves to every form of sensuality and luxury.

The children of the Vallabhācāryas are admitted to membership at the age of two, three, or four years. A rosary, or necklce (kaṇṭhī) of one hundred and eight beads[34], made of tulsī wood, is passed round their necks by the Mahārāja, and they are taught the use of the eight-syallabled prayer, 'Great Kṛishṇa is my soul's refuge' (Śrī-Krishṇah Śaraṇam mama).

The god worshipped is the Kṛishṇa form of Vishṇu, as he appeared in his boyhood, when, as a mere child, he gave himself up to childish mirth, and condescended to sport with the Gopīs or cowherdesses of Mathurā.

I was once present at a kind of revivalist camp-meeting near Allahābād, where a celebrated Hindū preacher addressed a large assemblage of people and magnified this condescension as a proof of Kṛishṇa's superiority of all other gods.

Then, again, used in the temples of the sect represent Kṛishṇa in the boyish period of his life (in the form called Bāla-Kṛishṇa), supposed to extend to his twelfth year. According to the higher Vaishṇava creed, Kṛishṇa's love for the Gopīs—themselves the wives of the cowherds—and the love of the Gopīs for Kṛishṇa are to be explained allegorically, and symbolize the longing of the human soul for union with the supreme (Brāhma-sambandha). When I have asked strict Vaishṇavas for an explanation of Krishṇa's alleged adulteries, I have always been told that his attachment to the Gopīs was purely spiritual, and that, in fact, he was only a child at the time of his association with them.

Yet it is certain that the followers of Vallabha interpreted that attachment in a gross and material sense. Hence their devotion to Krishṇa has degenerated into the most corrupt pratices. It will scarcely be believed that the male members of the sect often seek to win the favour of their god by wearing long hair and assimilating themselves to females; and even their spiritual chiefs, the Mahārājas, the successor of Vallabhācārya, sometimes simulate the appearance of women (that is, of Gopīs) when they led the worship of their followers.

But the real blot, or rather foul stain, which defaces and defiles the system, remains to be described. These Mahārājas have come to be regarded as representatives of Krishṇa upon earth, or even as actual incarnations or impersonalitions of the God. So that in the temples where the Mahārājās do homage to the idols, men and women do homage to the Mahārājās, prostrating themselves at their feet, offering them incense, fruits and flowers, and waving lights before them, as the Mahārājas, themselves do before the images of the Gods. One mode of worshipping the boyish Kṛiṣhṇa is by swinging his images in swings. Hence, in every district presided over by a Mahārāja, the women are accustomed to worship not Krishṇa but the Mahārāja by swinging him in pendent seats. The Pān-supārī ejected from his mouth, the leavings of his food, and the very dust on which he has walked, are eagerly accepted by his devotees, while they also drink the water rinsed from his garments, and that used in the washing of his feet, which they call Caraṇāmṛita, 'feet nectar'. Others, again, worship his wooden shoes, or prostrate themselves before his seat (gādī) and his painted portraits. Nay, infinitely worse than all this: it is believed that the best mode of propitiating the god Kṛishṇa in heaven is by ministering to the sensual appetites of his successors and vicars upon earth. Body, soul and property (in popular language *tan*, *man*, *dhan*) are to be wholly made over to them in a peculiar rite called Self-devotion (samarpaṇa), and women are taught to believe that highest bliss will be secured to themselves and their families by the caresses of Kṛishṇa's representatives.

The profligacy of the Mahārājas was exposed in the celebrated trail of the Mahārāja libel case, which came before the Supreme Court of Bombay on the January, 1862. The evidence given, and the judgement of the judges, did act as some check on the licentius practices of the sect, but it is still held to represent the worst and most corrupt phase of the Vaishṇava religion.

Sect founded by Caitanya

The fourth principal sect of Vāiṣhṇavas is found in Bengal. They are the followers of a celebrated teacher named Caitanya, and their precepts and practise have a close community with those of the Vallabhācāryars already described.

I believe it is pretty certain that Chaitanya was born at Nadīya (=Navadvīpa) in Bengal in the year 1485 of our era, two years after Luther in Europe. His father was an orthodox Brāhman named Jagannāth Miśrā. His mother was the daughter of Nīlāmbar Chakravartī. Since Chaitanya is held to have been an incarnation of Kṛishṇa verious prodigies are described as having marked his first appearance in the world. He was thirteen months in the womb. Then soon after birth, at the end of an eclipse, a number of holy men (among whom was his future disciple Advaita) arrived at the house of his parents to do homage to the new-born child, and to present him with offerings of rice, fruits, gold and silver. In his childhood he resembled the young Kṛishṇa in condesecending to boyish sports (līlā). Yet his intellect was so acute that he rapidly acquired a complete knowledge of Sanskṛit grammer and literature. His favourite subject of study were the Vaishṅava sacred books, consisting of the Bhāgavata-purāṇa, and the Bhagavad-gītā.

Yet Chaitanya, notwithstanding his devotion of religious study, did not shrink from what every Hindū believes to be a sacred obligation—the duty of marrying a wife, and becoming a householder (grihastha). He even married again when his first wife died from a snake-bite. At the age of twenty-five (A.D. 1509), he resolved to abandon all wordly connections, and give himself up to a religious life. Accordingly, like Vallabhāchārya and at about the same period, he commenced a series of pilgrimages. His travels occupied six years, and he is known to have visited some of the most celebrated shrines of India, especially those of Bānares, Gayā, Mathurā, Śrīrangam, and ultimately the temples of Jagannāth at Purī in Orissa.

Having thus prepared himself for his mission, he addressed himself to the real work of preaching and propagating his own view of the Vāishṇava creed. It is noteworthy that just about the time when Luther was agitating the minds of men in Europe, Chaitanya was stirring the hearts of the people of Bengal. After making many converts he seems to have appointed his two most eminent followers, Advaita and Nityānanda, to preside over his disciples in that part of India. He himself settled for twelve years at Cuttak in Orissa. There he lived for the rest of his life in close proximity to the great temple of Jagannāth, and contributed to the reputation of the shrine by his presence at the annual festivals.

His success as a preacher was remarkable. Even his oponents were attracted by the persuasiveness of his manner and the magnetic power of his eloquence. The lower classes flocked to him by thousands. Nor was their admiration of his surprising. The first principle he inculcated was that all the faithful worshippers of Kṛishṇa (=Vishṇu) were to be treated as equals. Caste was to be subordinated to faith in Kṛishṇā[35]. 'The mercy of God,' said Chaitanya, 'regards neither tribe nor family.'

By thus proclaiming social equality he secured popularity. In this respect he wisely imitated the method of Buddhists and Śāktas. The doctrine of the later, who abounded everywhere in Bengal, was that magical powers might be acquired (Śakti) in nature, personified as Śiva's wife. They believe that the male principle, personified as the male god Śiva, the great Reproducer, was helpless in the work of Reproduction without the energizing action of the female principle. Hence the union of the sexes was thought by some to be typical of a great cosmical mystery. This will be more fully explained in my book on Śāktism.

Chaitanya professed to oppose these Śākta doctrines, both as tending to licentious practices, and as ignoring the supermacy of the God Vishṇu over Śiva. Yet his system, like that of Vallabha, had a tendency in the same direction. He taught that the devotion of the soul to Viṣhṇu was to be symbolised under the figure of human love. '"Thou art dear to my heart, thou art part of my soul," said a young man to his loved one; "I love thee, but why, I know not." So ought the worshipper to love Krishṇa, and worship him for his sake only. Let him offer all to God, and expect no remuneration. He acts like a trader who asks for a return.' Such are the words of a modern exponent of the Vāishṇava system.

I have already pointed out that the idea of faith (bhaktī) as a means of salvation, which was formally taught by the authors of the Bhāgavad-gītā, Bhāgavata-purāṇa and Śāṇḍilya-sūtra, was scarcely known in early times. The leading doctrine of the Vedic hymns and Brāhmaṇas is that works (karma), especially as represented by the performance of sacrifices (yajña), constitute the shortest pathway to beatitude, while the Upanishads insist mainly on abstract meditation and divine knowledge (jñāna) as the true method. Chaitanya affirmed that faith and devotion—displayed by complete submission of the soul to Kṛishṇa—was the only road to heaven. Faith, in fact, superseded all other duties. 'Whatever is accomplished by works, by penance, by divine knowledge, by suppression of the passions, by abstract meditation, by charity, by virtue, by other excellences all this is effected by faith in me. Paradise, Heaven, supreme beatitude, union with the godhead,—every wish of the heart is obtainable by faith in me.' Such are Kṛishṇa's own words acording to the belief of Chaitanya and other Viashṇava teachers. (Bhāgavata-purāṇa XI.)

But the devotional feelings of Krishṇa's votaries are supposed to be susceptible of five phases, or rather, perhaps, to be exhibited in five different ways, which are thus enumerated:- 1. Calm contemplation of the godhead (Śānti); 2. Active servitude (dāsya); 3. A feeling of personal friemdship (sākhya); 4. A feeling of filial attachment like that of a child for its parent (vātsalya); 5. A feeling of tender affection like that of a girl for her lover (mādhurya).

The last of these is held to be the highest feeling. Indeed, Chaitanya taught that the great aim of every worshipper of Kṛishṇa ought to be to lose all individuality and self-consciousness in ecstatic union with the god. To bring about this condition of intense religious fervour various practices were enjoined—for example, incessant repetition of the deity's name (nāma-kīrtana), singing (saṅkīrtana), music, dancing, or movements of the body allied to dancing, such as were also practised by certain Śaiva devotees[36]. Chaitanya was himself in the constant habit of swooning away in paroxysms of esctatic emotion, which at last affected his reason. His biographers assert that in one of these states he was translated directly to Vishṇu's heaven (Vaikuṇtha). According to some accounts he ended his life by walking into the sea near Puri in Orissa, fancying he saw a beatific vision of Krishṇa sporting on the waves with his favourite Gopīs. Certain it is that he disappeared in a mysterious manner about A.D. 1527, at the age of forty-two.

Then happened what has constantly taken place in the religious history of India. Men of high aspirations, who have laboured for the revival or reformation of religion, and received homage as inspired teachers from crowds of disciples during life, have been worshipped as actual deities at death. The only question in the minds of Chaitanya's devoted followers was as to whether he was a full manifestation of the Supreme Being (Kṛishṇa) or only a descent of a portion of his essence. The difficulty seems to have been settled by deciding that Chaitanya was none other than very Kṛishṇa incarnate, and that his two principal disciples, Advaita and Nityāṅanda, were manifestatins of portions of the same deity. These three leaders of the sect are therefore called the three great lords (Prabhus). They constitute the sacred traid of this phase of Vaishṇavism.

But a fourth leader, named Hari-dās, who during his lifetime was a companion of Chaitanaya, is worshipped as a separate divinity in Bengal. Indeed, all the living successors and the present leaders of the sect, called Gosāins (=Gosvāmins), are venerated as little less than deities by the Vāishṇavas of this school. For the worship of living religious leaders and teachers (usually called by the general name Gūru) is a marked feature of this as of all forms of Vāishṇavism. The Gūru with Vāishṇavas is far more than a teacher, and even more than a mediator between God and men. He is the present god—the visible living incarnation of the deity.

His anger and favour make themselves instantly felt. He is on that account even more feared and honoured than the very God of whom he is the representatives and embodiment.

Another marked feature of the system is the extraordinary value attached to the repetition of Kṛiṣhṇa's names, especially of his name Harī. The mere repititive process of constantly repeating this name Hari—though the mind be perfectly vacant or fixed on some other object—secures admission to Vishṇu's heaven. Nothing else is needed. All religious ceremonies are comparatively useless. Hārīdās, is said to have retired to a secluded place in a wood for the purpose of repeating the world Hārī 300,000 times daily. Even a blasphemous repetition of Kṛiṣhṇa's name is believed by his followers to be quit sufficient to secure final beatitude. Indeed the Pandits of the Marātha country affirm that there is a form of devotion called Virodha-bhakti, which consists in a man's cursing the deity with the sole object of achieving the supreme bliss of being utterly annihilated by him, and so reabsorbed into the god's essence.

It is related of a certain wicked Godless man that he had a son named Nārāyaṇa (one of the principal names of Vishṇu). On his death-bed, and just before breathing his last, the father called out his son's name without the most remote intention of invoking the God. The effect was that Yama's messengers, who stood ready to convey the reprobate's soul to a place of punishment, were obliged to make way for the emissaries of Vishṇu, who carried the spirit off in triumph to the god's paradise.

A great many treatises (such as the Chaitanya-Charitāmrita written by Kṛishṇa-dās in 1590) have been composed by the disciples of Chaitanya in support of his tenets. These works are in high repute in Bengal.

The process of worshipping the images of Kṛishṇa has many points of resemblance with, that of Saivism.

The idol of the god Kṛishṇa first undergoes a process of being roused from its supposed nocturnal slumbers by the attendent priests, who invoke the deity by name. Then a respectful offering of water in a boat-shaped vesel is made to it. Next the whole idol is bathed and holy water poured over it from a small perforated metal lotā. Then the attendent priest standing near aplies sandal-paste (Chandana) with his finger to the idol's forehead and limbs, and, taking a brush, paints the face with a bright colouring substance, probably saffron. Next, the idol is dressed and decorated with costly clothes and ornaments. Then the priest burns camphor and incense and waves lights before the image, at the same time ringing a small bell (ghaṇṭā). Then flowers (pushpa) and the leaves of the sacred tulsī plant are offered, followed by an oblation of food (naivedya), consisting of cooked rice with sugar. Next water is taken out of a small metal vessel with a spoon and is presented for sipping (ācāmana). The god is of course supposed to consume the food or feast on its aroma, receiving at the end of the meal an offering of betel for the supposed cleansing of the mouth after eating, and a spoonful more water for a second sipping. Finally the priest prostrates himself before the idol, and that terminates the whole ceremony by putting the god comfortably to sleep for the day.

In the evening the process of walking, undressing, and redressing the image is repeated, but without bathing. Flowers and food are again offered, prayers and texts are intoned, a musical service is performed, and the idol put to sleep once more.

The cooked food offered to the idol is ultimately eaten by the priests. In large temples it is also distributed to the worshippers, who receive it eagerly as divine nutriment (praśad), and at some places (for example at a particular temple in Banaras) considerable portions are sold at high prices to outside applicants. The water in which the idol is washed is called tīrtha, and is drunk as holy water.

Foot Notes

1. These, of course, are capable of subdivision.
2. It is worthy of note that Ātman (which is the earlier word for the one Spirit of the Universe) is masculine, while Brahman, the later word, is neuter. The etymology of Ātman is doubtful. Some derive it from *at*, to move; others form *ah*, connected with *aham*, I; others from *vī*, top blow at the wind; and others (as we have seen) from *an*, to breathe (compare p. 20). No doubt Ātman was originally the breath of life-the breath that animates the Universe and man's living soul-the power in which and by which man lives, and moves, and has his being. In the well-known hymn *Rig-veda* I. 115, I, the Sun (Sūryaḥ)-interpreted by advanced Pandits to mean the Supreme Being-is called the Soul(Ātman) of the Universe (that is, of all that moves and is immovable); and in the Taittirīya Āraṅyaka, VIII. I, the ethereal element called Ākāśa (supposed to fill and pervade the Universe and to be vehicle of life) is said to be produced from Ātman. The name Brahman, which is the most usual name for the one Spirit of the Universe in later writings, was at first connected with the spiritual power inherent in the Vedic hymns and prayers. The Veda itself is often called Brahmā, and described as the breath (ucchvasita) of the Supreme.
3. There can be no doubt that the anti-idolatrous sect founded by Kabīr (to be afterwards noticed) grew out of Vaishṇavism.
4. There are seven lower regions, viz. Atāla, Vitāla, Sutāla, Rasātala, Talātala, Mahātala, and Pātāla; above which are the seven Lokās or worlds, called Bhūr (the earth), Bhuvar, Svar, Mahaḥ, Janaḥ, Tapaḥ, and Brāhma or Satya. Sometimes the first three of these, the earth (Bhū), atmoshpere (Bhuvar), and heaven (Svar), are supposed to comprehend all the worlds.
5. Described as a peculiar twist or curl of the hair. In one form of Kṛiṣhṇa (as Vithobā in the Marāṭha country) his breast has a foot-mark, believed to be the indelible impress

of the blow from the sage Bhṛigu's foot.

6. One account described the sacred conch-shell as thrown up by the sea when churned by the gods and demons. Another account makes Vishṇu's shell consist of the bones of the demon Pañcajana. According to the Vishṇu-purāṇa (V.21), this demon lived in the form of a conch-shell under the ocean. Kṛishṇa (Vishṇu) plunged into the waters, killed him, took the shell which constitutes his bones, and ever afterwards used it for a horn. When sounded it fills the demon-hosts with dismay, animates the gods, and annihilates unrighteousness.' Vishṇu is believed to take such delight in this shell, that a small shell of the same species is used in pouring holy water over his idols and symbols in the performance of his worship. It is also frequently branded on the arms of his worshippers.
7. The Svastika mark is a kind of curtailed form of this wheel, and may be supposed to consist of four spokes and a portion of the circumference, left to denote the direction in which it must turn to symbolize the Sun's course in the heavens. This conjecture, which I formed long ago, is confirmed by Mr. Edw. Thomas's article in the *Numismatic Chronicle*.
8. The names of some of the chief demons thus destroyed by Vishṇu (or Kṛishṇa identified with Vishṇu) are Madhu, Kaṇsa, Bāna, Bali, Mura, etc.
9. In some parts of Southern India Garuḍa is an object of worship. I frequently came across images of him in the galleries of Vaishṇava temples. He is the son of Kaśyapa and Vinatā, and hence Aruṇa the Dawn, regarded as charioteer of the Sun, is his younger brother. Most of the Hindū deities are described as associated with or attended by their own favourite animals, which they sometimes use as vehicles (vāhana). Brahmā is attended by a goose or swan (haṇsa); Śiva by bull; Kārttikeya or Skanda by a peacock; Indra by an elephant; Yama by a buffalo (manisha); Kāma 'god of love,' by a parrot; Gaṇeśa by a rat; Agni by a ram; Varuṇa by a fish; Durgā by a tiger. Serpents

are associated with both Śiva and Vishṇu.

10. Of course the greter number of the names are simply epithets. The Muhammadams reckon ninety-nine names and epithets of God, and make the repetition (zikr) of them a work of enormous religious merit. In the same way the Jews attach great efficacy to the repetition of the Divine epithets. Christianity reckons, I believe, about ninety epithets of Chirst, but no Christian thinks of repeating them as a meritorious excercise. Aristotle, I think, enumerates more than a hundred names and epithets applicable to Zeus; but the Greeks and Romans do not appear to have believed in any religious advantages attending their mechanical recital.

11. I notice several repetitions of the same name in the catalogue; for instance, Āditya, Sthāṇu, Srashṭṛi.

12. Other remarkable names and epithets of Vishṇu are the following:- 'the Bridge' (Setuḥ), 'the Guide (Netā), 'the All' (Sarvaḥ), 'the Refuge' (Śaraṇam), 'the Friend' (Suhṛid), 'the Affectionate '(Vatsalaḥ), 'the Benefactor' (Priya-kṛit), 'the Witness' (Sākshī), 'the Patient' (Sahishṇuh), 'the Peace-giver' (Śānti-daḥ), 'the Authority' (Pramāṇam), 'the Mystrius one' (Guhyaḥ), 'the Underlying-bodied one' (Amrita-vapuḥ), 'the Holy' (Brahmaṇyaḥ), 'the Winkless' (Animishaḥ), 'the Desired one' (Ishṭaḥ), 'the Who ?' (Kaḥ), 'the What' (Kim).

13. That is, the Manu of the present period—not to be confounded with Brahmā's grandson, the suppossed author of the well-known Law-book. The name Manu is from the root *man*, 'to think.'

14. When I asked any Indian Pandit how it was possible to believe in what to us appears an extravagant fable I was always told that it was simply allegorical, and only intended to typify the truth, that nothing valuable can be produced without extraordinary exertion.

15. This is one proof out of many that the drinking of wine and spirits was once not only common in India, but also sanctioned by religion. In Vedic times wine appears

to have been preserved in leathern bottles, see *Rig-veda* I. 191. 10 (Rājendralāla Mitra's *Essays*, VII). Unhappily the sect of Śāktas (see the appeal on Śāktism) may claim scriptural authority for their orgies, and appeal to the example of their Gods Śiva and Balarāma.

16. Two such bows are mentioned in Hindū mythology, one is property of Śiva and the other of Vishṇu. It was by bending Śiva's bow—which no other merely human suitor was able to do—that Rāma won Janaka's daughter Sitā (see Rāmayaṇa I. 57)
17. This would be the third age reckoning backwards, and is therefore called Tretā.
18. In paintings he is often represented with a peculiar greensih complexion. The exact significance of Chandra is not clear.
19. Kṛishṇa was no doubt a powerful chief of the Yādhva tribe, who mere probably Rājputs occupying a district of Central Indian south of Mathurā and east of the Yamuna. The real date of his birth, though kept as a holy day and holiday throughout a great part of India cannot be fixed with any more certainly than that of Rāma; but in all probability he lived in more recent times than Rāma.
20. The two most powerful lines of Indian princes, those of Oudh and Rājputāna, were careful to trace back their pedigree to superhuman origins, the former claiming to be the Sun-god and the latter the Moon-god as their primeval progenitors.
21. Compare nore. The day of his birth is called Janmāshṭamī. It is kept on the eighth day of the dark half of the month Bhādra in some places, and of Śrāvaṇa in others.
22. In Buddhism, there is the future Buddha; in Islām the Mahdī. The succession of Buddhas may be compared to that of Vishṇu's descents.
23. This is because there are one hundred and eight chief names of Kṛishṇa as the Supreme Being.
24. This is given in the *Sarva-darśana-sangraha* as one of Rāmānuja's precepts. Compare a similar precept at the

end of the *Kaṭhopanishad*. I read an excellent sermon on this text delivered by Professor Bhāṇḍārkar in the house of prayer of the Prārthanā-Samāj in Bombay.

25. The twenty-ninth Sūtra of Śāṇḍilya (translated by Prof. E.B.Cowell) mentions a sage Kāśyapa who appears to have held doctrines coinciding to a certain extent with those of Rāmānuja.

26. See *Sarva-darśana-saṅgraha* (Prof. A. E. Gough's translation of the Rāmānuja system), p. 79.

27. The Sātāni branch of the Rāmānujas is not a separate school. It consists of a body of Śūdras who are opposed to Brāhmanical usages. It represents, in fact, the low-caste or out-caste converts to Vaishṇavism. It is among the Rāmānuja Vaishṇavas what the Lingāit sect is among Śaivas (see p. 88).

28. The Ten-galais quote a verse of Vṛiddha-Manu, which declares that if any woman, whether unmarried or widowed, shave her head, she will be condemned to dwell in the hell called Raurava for one thousand times ten million ages.

29. Caste-rules are now as essential part of religion, but there is reason to believe that they were once merely matters of social convenience. Many of them probably originated in the need of sanitary precautions. Nothing is so necessary for the preservation of health in India as attention to the purity of water.

30. I repeatedly questioned some of the more intelligent followers of Madhva I met in the South of India as to the exact distinction between his views and those of Rāmānuja, but no one was able to give me any very satisfactory reply.

31. See pp. 88, 90 of Cowell and Gough's *Sarva-darśana-saṅgraha*.'

32. This was very much the doctrine of the Kabbalists, who equally field that nothing could be produced from nothing. It resembles also the theory of the Stoics.

33. The Śuddhāvaita or 'pure Non-duality' doctrine—which

he is said to have held in contradistinction to the Viśishṭādvaita of Rāmānuja—is not very clearly explined in the books of the sect.

34. These represents the 108 chief names of Kṛishṇa as the Supreme Being, to match which a similar number of epithets are applied to the successors of Vallabha.

35. This was his theory, but among his numerous followers of the present day the doctrine of equality does not overcome caste-feeling and caste-observances except during religious services. The food presented to the idol of Jagannāth is distributed to all castes alike, and eaten by all indiscriminately at the annual festival.

36. These correspond to the Zikr religious dancing of the Muhammadan dervishes. For even Islām has its devotees who aim at religious ecstasy, resorting expedients very similar to those of the Chaitanyas. I have been twice present at the weekly services of the Cairo dervishes. One sect repeat the name of God with violent ejaculations and contortions of the body, while another fraternity whirl themselves round till they swoon away in the intensity of their religious fervour.

Excerpted from *Indian Wisdom* by M.M. Williams. Published by Cosmo Publications, New Delhi.

TWO

VĀIṢHṆĀVISM: MINOR SECTS AND REFORMING THEISTIC MOVEMENTS

The discussion on Vaishnavism can not be complete without giving some account of its more important minor sects, as well as of certain reforming theistic movements which may be said to have grown out of it. We may begin with the:

Sect founded by Nimbārka or Nimbāditya

This is perhaps one of the oldest of the known minor sects. Its founder Nimbārka or Nimbāditya, whose followers are sometimes called Nīmānandis, sometimes Nimāvats, is held to have been identical with the astronomer Bhāskarāchārya, who flourished about the twelfth century. The poet Jayadeva, who is also supposed to have lived in twelfth century, may have been his desciple. If so, it is certain that the disciple did more than his master to promote the doctrine of devotion to Kṛishṇa. In Jayadeva's mystical poem, called the Gita-govinda (compared by some to the Song of Solomon), are described the loves of Kṛishṇa and Gopis (wives and daughters of the Cowherds), and especially of Kṛishṇa and Rādhā, as typical of the longing of the human soul for union with the divine.

Others again believe Nimbārka to have been an actual

incarnation of the Sun-god, and maintain that he derived his name of 'Nimb-tree-Sun' from having one day stopped the course of the sun's disk, dislodged it from the heavens, and confined it for a brief season in Nimb (Nīm) tree. Acccording to Hindū ideas, this remarkable miracle was worked for no unworthy or insufficient purpose. It enabled Nimbārka to offer food just before sunset to a holy guest whose religious vows prevented his eating after dark.

No noteworthy doctrines distinguish Nimbārka's creed, except, perhaps, that his followers, who are not very numerous, are particular to worship the goddess Rādhā in conjunction with Kṛishṇa.

Sect founded by Rāmānanda

Rāmānanda is said to have been born in the thirteenth century. The sect founded by him in the fourteenth century has many adherents in Gangetic India, especially around Agra. They are often called Rāmānandis or Ramavats, and are sometimes confounded with the Rāmānujas, the fact being that Ramananda was probably one of Ramanuja's disciples. The Rāmānanda Vāishṇavas, however, have distinctive doctrines of their own. they worship Vishṇu under the form of Rāma (the horo of the Rāmāyaṇa) either singly or conjointly with his wife Sītā, and they are not like the Rāmānujas, hyper-scrupulous about the privacy of their meals. Their favourite book is Bhaktamālā of Nābhāji—a work interesting for its biographies of certain Vaishṇavas and adherents of the sect, among whom are included two well-known poets, Sūrdās and Tulasīdās (commonly Tulsīdās). The former was blind. He wrote a vast number of stanzas in praise of Vishṇu, and is regarded as a kind of patron of blind men, especially if they roam about as wandering musicians.

Tulsīdās, whose verses are to this day household words in every town and rural district where the Hindī language is spoken, ranks as a poet of higher order. He was born near Citrakūṭa about A.D. 1544, and settled at Benares, where he become an enthusiastic worshipper of Rāma and Sītā.

Sect founded by Sahajānanda

In a large and populous city a man of evident ability and professed sanctity could not fail to attract attention. Soon Sahajānanda collected about his own person a little band of disciples, which rapidly multiplied into an army of devoted adherents. Some attribute his influence to a power of mesmerizing his followers, but he probably owed his success to a remarkable fascination of manner combined with consistency of moral character, and other qualities which singled him out for a leader. His desciples increased so repidly that the Brāhmans and magnates of Allahabad began to be jealous of his popularity. He was obliged to fly, and sought refuge at Jetalpur, twelve miles south of Ahmedābād. There he invited all the Brāhmans of the neighbourhood to the performance of a great sacrifice. The native officials no sooner heard of the proposed assemblage than, fearing a collision between his followers and other religious parties, they had him arrested on some frivolous pretext and thrown into prison. Such an act of tyranny defeated its own object. It excited universal sympathy, and increased his influence. He was soon released. Hymns were composed in which his merits were extolled. Verses were written descriptive of his sufferings. Couses were launched against the head of his persecutors.

Jetalpur then become the focus of a great religious gathering. Thousands flocked to the town and enrolled themselves as the followers of Sahajananda, who took the name of Swamī-Nārāyana.

Bishop Heber, in his *Indian Journal*, gives the following interesting account of an interview with him at this period of his carreer:—

About eleven o'clock I had the expected visit from

Svami-Nārāyana.

The holy man was a middle-sized, thin, plain-looking person about my own age, with a mild and diffident expression of countenance, but nothing about him indicative of any extraordinary talent. He came in somewhat different style from all I had expected, having with him nearly two hundred horsemen. When I considered that I had myself an escort of more than fifty horse I could not help smiling, though my sensations were in some degree painful and humiliating at the idea of two religious teachers meeting, at the head of little armies, and filling the city which was the scene of their interview with the rattling of quivers, the clash of shields, and the tramp of the war-horse. Had our troops been opposed to each other, mine, though less of arms and discipline. But in moral grandeur what a difference was there between his troop and mine ! Mine neither knew me nor cared for me, though they escorted me faithfully. The guards of Svami-Narayana were his own disciples and enthusiastic admirers men who had volunatarily repaired to hear his lessons, who now took a pride in doing him honour, and who would cheerfully fight to the last drop of blood rather than suffer a fringe of his garment to be handled roughly. In my own parish of Hodnet there were once, perhaps, a few honest countrymen who felt something like this for me, but how long a time must elapse before a Christian minister in India can hope to be thus loved and honoured!—Chap. xxv.

It soon became clear to Sahajananda that the success of his future operations would depend on the consolidation of his party. He therefore retired with his followers to the secluded village of Wartal, where he erected a temple to Nārāyana (otherwise Kṛishṇa, or Vishṇu, as the supreme Being) associated with the goddess Lakṣhmī. It was from this central locality that his crusade against the licentious habits of the Vallabhācarys was principally carried on. His watchword seem to have been 'devotion to Kṛiṣhṇa' (as the Supreme Being) with observance of duty and purity of life.

He was in the habit of making periodical tours in Gujarat, like a bishop visiting his diocese. It was in one of these that Svami-Narayana was struck down by fever at Gadada in Kathiawar, where he died.

His disciples now number more than 200,000. They are broadly divided into two classes—Sadhus, 'holy men,' and 'Grihasthas,' 'householders.' These correspond to clergy and laity, the former, who are all celibates, being supported by the latter. Those Sadhus who are Brahmans are called Brahmacharis. Of these there are about 300 at Wartal, the whole body of Sadhus or holy men, numbering about 1,000. A still lower order is called pala. Of these there are about 500.

The two principal temples of the sect are at Wartal (for Sanskrit Vrittalaya or better Vratalaya, 'abode of religious observances') about four miles to the west of Baroda and Ahmedabad. The former is the most important and best endowed, but both are presided over by Maharajas neither of whom is willing to yield the precedence to the other. Jealousies are already springing up between them, Probably, in process of time, a schism will take place, and perhaps two antagonistic parties be formed, as in the other Vaishnava sects.

The following is narrated by M.M. Williams in his *Indian Wisdom:*

> In company with the Collector of Kaira I visted the Wartal temple on the day of the Purnima or full moon of the month Karttika—the most popular festival of the whole year. The Maharaja greeted us at the Boravi station of the Baroda railway with a choice of conveynces—an elephant, a bullock carriage, a palanquin and four horses, with a mounted guard. I chose the palanquin

and found myself moving comfortably forward, while my companion's vehicle oscillated violently in response to the inequalities of the road. The Svami-Nārāyana sect are a wealthy community, but clearly object to spend their money on improving their access to their chief temple. One reason for this may be that a shrine's inaccessibility enhances the merit of pilgrimage.

We were met at the entrance to the court of the temple (maṁdir) by the Māhāraja himself, attended by his minister—an old Brāhṁachari, or unmarried Brāhṁan. The temple dedicated to Lakshmi-Narayana, erected about sixty years ago, is a handsome structure. It has the usual lofty cupolas, and stands in the centre of a courtyard, formed by the residences of the Māhāraja and his attendants, the great hall of assembly, and other building.

We were conducted by the Māhāraja through a crowd of at least ten thousand persons, who thronged the quadrangle and all the approaches to the temple. They were waiting to be admitted to the ceremony of the day—one object that had drawn so many people to the spot the privilege of Darshana; that is, of seeing and adoring the idol. It was a moment of intense excitement. Let a man but down before the jewelled image on this anniversary of its manifestation to the multitude, and the blessing of the God attends him for the whole year. The vast concourse swayed to and fro like the waves of the troubled sea, each man vociferating to his neighbours. I could not help thinking of our apparent helplessness in the surging crowd, and asking myself how two solitary Europeans would be likely to fare, if from some accidental circumstance, the religious fanaticism of a myriad of excited Hindus were to break loose and vent itself upon us.

But the ten thousand people were docile as children. At a signal from the Māhāraja they made a lane for us to pass, and we entered the temple by a handsome flight of steps. The interior is surrounded by idol shrines. On the the occasion of the present festival the principal images were almost concealed from view by rich vestments and jewellry.

The two principal shrines have three figures. One of them has an idol of Kṛishṇa in his character of Ranchor, 'deliverer from evil'—a form of Kṛishṇa specially worshipped at Dvārikā and throughout Gujrāt. An image of Nārāyaṇa (Vishṇu as the Supreme Being) is in the middle; and Lakshmī, consort of Vishṇu, is on the right. A gong to be struck in the performance of worship (pūjā) hangs suspended before the shrine. The other principal sanctuary has Kṛishṇa in the middle, his favourite Rādhā on the right, and Svāmi-Nārāyaṇa, the founder of the sect, on the left. The latter is here worshipped, like other great religious leaders, as an incarnation of a portion of Vishṇu—that is, he is held to be one of the numerous Narāvatāras or descents of parts of the god's essence in the bodies of men. In an adjacent shrine are his bed and clothes, the print of his foot, and his wooden slippers.

We were next conducted to the Sabhā-maṇḍapa, or great hall of assembly, on one side of the quadrangle. Here about three thousand of the chief members of the sect, including a number of the Sādhus or clergy, were waiting to receive us. Chairs were placed for us in the centre of the hall, and before us, seated on the ground, with their legs folded under them in the usual Indian attitude, were two rows of about thirty of the oldest Sādhus, three or four of whom had been actually contemporaries of Svāmi-Nārāyaṇa. These old men were delighted when we questioned them as to their personal knowledge of their founder. The only inconvenience was that they all wanted to talk together. I fell indisposed to check their garrulity, but the mahārāja interposed and invited us to another spacious hall in the story above, where people were assembled to greet us. The regular Darbar or formal reception took place in this room. Here we were garlanded with flowers, be sprinked with rosewater, and presented with fruits, sweet-meat, and pan-supari, in the usual manner. I found the Pandits we versed in Sanskrit. One or two astonished me by the fluency with which they spoke it, and by their readiness in answering the difficult questions when I tested their knowledge.

The Māhāraja's last act was to conduct us to an adjacent building, used as a lodging-house (dharma-sala) for the clergy. On the present anniversary at least six hundred or these good men were collected in long spacious galleries called Āsramas (places of retreat). They were all dressed alike in plain salmon-coloured clothes, each man being located in a small separated space not more than seven feet long, by three or four broad. Above head, neatly arranged in racks, were his spare clothes, water-jar, &c. When we were introduced to the six hundred Sadhus they were all standing upright, motionless, and silent. At night they lie down on the ground in the same narrow space. These holy men are all celibtes. They have abandoned all worldly ties, that they may go forth unencumbered to desseminate the doctrines of their founder. They itinerate inpairs, to cheer, support, and keep watch on each other. They travel on foot, undergoing many privations and hardships and taking with them nothing but a staff, the clothes on their back, their daily food, their water-jar, and their book of instructions. They may be seen here and there in the ordinary coarse salmon-coloured dress of ascetics, striving to win disciples by personal example and persuasion, rather than by controversy. Surely other proselyting societies might gain some useful hints by a study of their method.

What I saw of their whole system convinced me that the Swamī-Nārāyanas are an energetic body of men, and their sect an advancing one. Notwithstanding the asceticism of their clergy, the leading members of the community have a keen eye to worldly wealth and the acquisition of land, and are perhaps not over-scrupulous in carrying out their plans of aggrandisement. Without doubt the tendency of their doctrines is towards purity of life, which is supposed to be effected by suppression of the passions (udasa), and complete devotion to the Supreme Being in his names of Nārāyana, Viṣhṇu, and Kṛishṇa. In an honest desire to purify the Vāishṇava faith the sect has done and is doing much good; but there can be no question that its doctrines, like its gods, its idols, and its sectarian marks, are part and parcel of genuine Vāishṇavism. At any rate the system lacks the true vivifying regenerating force which can alone maintain it in vigour.

After my discussions with the Pandits I was presented with their Siksha-patri, or manual of instructions, written in Sanskrit (with a long commentary), and constituting the religious directory of the sect. It was compiled by their founder, with the aid of a learned Brahman named Dinanath, and is a collection of two hundred and twelve precepts—some original some extracted from Manu and other sacred Sastras, and many of them containing high moral sentiments. Every educated member of the sect appeared to know the whole collection by heart.

Some of the verses were recited to me by the Pandits in the original Sanskrit, and as they are calculated to give a fair idea of the purer side of modern Vāishṇavism, I here append a literal translation of a few selected specimens. The figures at the end of each precept refer to the number of the verses in the Siksha-patrī.

No disciples of mine must ever intentionally kill any living thing whatever, not even a flea or the most minute insect (11).

The killing of any animal for the purpose of sacrifice to the gods is forbidden by me. Abstaining from injury is the highest of all duties (12).

Suicide at a sacred place of pilgrimage, from religious motives or from passion, is prohibited (14).

No flesh meat must ever be eaten, no spirituous or vinous liquor must ever be frunk, not even as medicine(15).

All theft is prohibited, even under pretence of contributing to religious objects (17).

No male or female followers of mine must ever commit adultery (18).

No false accusation must be laid against any one from motives of self- interest (20).

Profane language against the Gods, sacred places, Brāhmans holy men and women, and the Vedās, must never be used (21).

A truth which causes serious injury to one's self or others need not be told. Wicked men, ungrateful people, and persons in love are to be avoided. A bride must never be accepted(26).

Holy men should patiently bear abusive language, or even beating, from evil-minded persons, and wish good to them (210).

They should not play at any games of chance, nor act as informers or spies; they should never show love of self, or nudue partiality for their relations (202).

Wives should honour their husbands as if they were gods, and never offend them with improper language, though they be diseased, indignent, or imbecile (159).

Widows should only eat one meal a day, and should sleep on the ground (168).

Every day let a man awake before sunrise, and, after

calling on the name of Kṛiṣhṇa proceed to perform the rites of bodily purification (49).

Having seated himself in some place apart, let him cleanse his teeth, and then having bathed with pure water, purt on two well washed garments,one an under garment and the other an upper (50).

My male followers should then make the vertical mark (emblematical of the footprint of Vishṇu or Kriṣhṇa) with the round spot inside it (symbolival of Lakshmi) on their foreheads. Their wives should only make the circular mark with red powder of saffrom (52).

Those who are initiated into the proper worship of Kriṣhṇa should always wear on their neacks two rosaries made of Tulsi wood, one for Kriṣhṇa and the other for Rādhā (4).

After regaging inmental worwship let them reverently bow down before the pictures of Radha and Kriṣhṇa, and repeat the eight syllabled prayer to Kṛishṇa (Sri-Kṛishṇah saranam mama, 'Great Kṛiṣhṇa is my soul's refuge') as many times as possible. Then let them apply themselves to secular affairs (54).

Devotion to Kṛiṣhṇa unattended by the performance of duties must on no account be practised (39)

The duties of one's own class and order must never be abandoned, nor the duties of others meddled with (24).

Nowhere, except in Jagan nathpuri, must cooked food or water be accepted from a person of low caste, though it be the remains of an offering to Kṛiṣhṇa (19).

Duty (dharma) is that good practice which is enjuined both by the Veda (Sruti) and by the law (Smriti) founded on the Veda. Devotion (bhakti) is intense love for Kṛiṣhṇa accompanied with a due sense of his glory (103)

An act promising good reward, but involving departure from proper duties, must never be committed (73)

If by the promising good reward, but involving departure from proper duties, must never be committed (73).

If by the great men of former days anything unbecoming has been done, their faults must not be imitated, but only their good deeds (74).

If knowingly or unintentionally any sin, great or small, be committed, the proper penance must be performed according to ability (92).

Even day all my followers should go to the Temple of God, and there repeat the names of Kriṣhṇa (63).

The story of his life should be listened to with the greatest reverence, and hymns in his praise should be sung on festive days (64).

All males and females who go to Kriṣhṇa's temple should keep separate and not touch each other (40).

Vishṇu, Ṡivā, Gana-pati, (or Gāṇesa), Pāravati, and the sun; these five deities should be honoured with worship (84).

Nāṛayana and Ṡiva should be equally regarded as part of one and the same Supreme Spirit, since both have been declared in the Vedās to be forms of Brāhṁa(47).

On no account let it be supposed that difference in forms (or names) makes any difference in the identity of the deity (112).

That which abides within the living human spirit in the character of its internal regulator (antaryamitaya) should be regarded as the self-existent Supreme Being who assigns a recompense to every act. (107).

That being, known by various names—such as the glorious

Kṛiṣhṇa, Param Brahma, Bhagavan, Purushottaama—the cause of all manifestations, is to be adored by us as our one chosen deity (108).

Having perceived, by abstract meditation, that the spirit is distinct from its three dodies (*viz.* the gross, subtle, and causal bodies) and that it is a portion of the one Spriti of the Universe (Brahma), every man ought to worship Kriṣhṇa by means of that soui at all times (116).

Towards him alone ought all worship to be directed by every human being on the earth in every possible manner. Nothing else except faith (bhakti) in him can procure salvation (113).

The philosophical doctrine approved by me is the Visishtadvaita (of Rāmānuja), and the desired heavenly abode is Goloka. There to worship Kriśhṇa and be united with him as the Supreme Soul is to be considered salvation (121).

The twice-born should perform at the proper seasons, and according to their means, the twelve purificatatory rites (sanskara), the (six) daily duties, and the Srāddhā offereings to the spirits of departed ancestors (91)

The eleventh day of the waxing and waning moon should be observed as fasts, also the birthday of Kṛiṣhṇa; also the night of Śivā (Siva-ratri) with revoicings during the day (79)...

A pilgrimage to the Tirthas, or holy places,of which Dvarika (Kṛiṣhṇa's city in Gujarat) is the chief, should be performed according to rule. Alms giving and kind acts towards the poor should always be performed by all (83).

A tithe of one's income should be assigned to Kriṣhṇa; the poor should give a twentieth part (147).

Those males and females of my followers who will act

according to these directions shall certainly obtain the four great objects of all human desires - religious merit, wealth, pleasure, and beatitude (206).

We now pass on the reformed theistic sects founded by Kabir and Nanak.

Theistic Sect founded by Kabir

There can be no doubt that the teaching of Kabir exercised a most important influence throughout Upper India in the fifteenth and sixteenth centuries. That it formed that basis of the Sikh movement in the Panjab is clear from the fact that Kabir's sayings are constantly quoted by the Guru Nanak and his successors, the authors of the sacred writings, which constitute the sacred book (Grantha) of the Sikh religion.

Kabir was a weaver, and in all probability a Muslim by birth. He is believed to have lived partly at Banaras and partly at Magar, near Gorakhpur, in the reign of Sikandar Shah Lodi, between 1488 and 1512. According to a legend he was miraculously conceived by the virgin widow of a Brāhman. His name of Kabīr—an Arabic word meaning 'Great'—gives support to the now generally accepted opinion that he was originally a Muslim. But he never had any sympathy with Muhammadan intolerance and exclusivensess. It is certain that in the end he became a pupil of Rāmānanda, and for a time a true Hindū, and what is important to bear in mind, a true Vaishṇva who, like other Vaishṇavạ leaders, had much of the democratic, tolerant, and libral spirit. No wonder, then that he laboured to free the Vaishṇava creed from the useless and senseless incrustations with which it had become overlaid. But he did more than other Vaishṇava reformers. He denounced all idol-worship and taught Vaishṇ-avism as a form of strick monotheism. True religion, according to Kabīr, meant really nothing but devotion to one God, who is called by the name Vishṇu, or by synonyms of Vishṇu such as Rāma and Hari, or even by the names current among Muhammadans. For Kabīr, in his tolerance had no objection to regard Muhammadans as worshipping the same God under a diffrerent name. In this way he was the first to attempt a partial bridging of the gulf between Hindūism and Islām. Nor did he reject all the pantheistic ideas of Brāhmanism.

We have already noted how in India all phases of religious belief are constantly meeting and partially fusing into each other. Polytheism is continually sliding into, Monotheism Monotheism into Pantheism, and then again into Polytheism. Vaishṇavism and Śaivism in their universal receptivity are open to impressions from Islām; Islām, notwithstanding its exclusiveness, is adulterated with Vaishṇavism and Śaivism. Hence it happens that Vaishṇavism and Śaivism, however decidedly they may insist on the separete personality of the Godhead, are perpetually slipping back, like a broad wheel, into the old Pantheistic rut. And Islam, however uncompromising its view of the Unity of the Deity, has its school of Sufi philosophers, who hold opinion almost identical with those of the Vedanta Pantheists. It is no matter of wonder, therefore, that Kabir—while asserting the Unity of God, the Creator of the world, who is admitted to have attributes and qualities and to assume any shape at will also maintained that God and man are parts of one essence, and that 'both are in same manner everything that lives and moves and has being.'

Kabir's adherents—still very numerous in northern India—are generally called Kabir-panthis. His doctrines and precepts are embodied in the *Sudh-nidhan* and other Hindi works, as well as in the sikh Graṇtha. His succesors have added precepts of their own, many of which are attributed to Kabir. His alleged sayings are innumerable.

I here subjoin a few specimens:—

Hear my word; go not astray.
My word is from the first. Meditate on it every moment.
Without hearing the word, all is utter darkness. Without

finding the gateway of the world, all is utter darkness. Without finding th egateway of the word, man will ever go astray.

There are many words. Take the pith of them.

Lay in provender sufficient for the road while time yet serves. Evening comes on, the day is flown and nothing will be provided.

With the five elements is the abode of a great mystery. When the body is decomposed has any one found it ?

The word of the teacher is the guide.

That a drop falls into the ocean all can perceive; but that the drop and the oean are one, few can comprehend.

The dwelling of Kabir is on the peak of a mountain, and narow path leads to it.

No act of devotion can equal truth; no crime is so heinous as false hood; in the heart where truth abides, there is my abode.

Put a check upon the tongue; speak not much. Associate with the wise. Investigate the words of the teacher.

When the master is bling, what is to become of the acholar? When the blind leads the blind both will fall into the well.

It is evident from these examples that the key-note of Kabir's teaching was the duty of obeying spiritual teachers. He maintained, in fact, that every man was bound to search for a true and trustworthy spiritual pastor (Guru), and, having found one, to make him his master—to submit mind, conscience, and even body to his will and guidance. Yet he never claimed infallibility of his own utterances. He constantly warned his own disciples to investigate for themselves the truth of every word he uttered.

And this leads us to the religious system founded in the Panjab by Kabīir's most celebrated follower Nanak, about the time of Emperor Babar.

The Sikh Theistic Sect, founded by Nanak.

It is well known that certain sects of Christains call themselves 'brethren', to denote their relationship to each other and to their Head as members of a religious society typified by a family. Much in the same way the sect founded by Nanak styled themselves Sikhs or 'disciples' to express their close dependence on their teachers or Gurus. For if the 'diapassion' of Kabir's doctrine, and, in indeed, of all Vaishnava teaching, was, Hear the word of the Guru, the word of the Guru is the guide,' much more did Nanak insist on a similar submission. Literally interpreted, the Sanskrit terms Gūru (derived from the Sanskrit root *gri*, 'to utter words'), and Sishya—corrupted into Sikh,—meaning in Sanskrit! 'one who is to be instructed,' are merely correlatives like teacher and taught. Hence, the system might as suitably be called Guruism as Sikhism.

Great light has been thrown on its religious aspect by the labours of Professor Trumpp, of Munich. He was commissioned by the British Government to translate what is called the Ādi-Grańth, or first Sidh bible, and his work appeared with valuable introductory essays. It is not too much to say that we are now for the first time able to form an accurate idea of the true nature of one of the most interesting and important religious and political movements in the history of India.

In the light, therefore, of Professor Trumpp's investigations, and other scholars of the time I proceed to give a brief account of Nānak and the characteristic features of Nānak's teachings.

It appears to be well-ascertained fact that this great teacher was born, not in Lahore inself, but in a neighbouring village, called Talvandi, on the river Rāvī, not far from Lahore, in the year 1469, a few years before Chaitanya in Bengal and Martin Luther in Europe. Of course the verious biographies of Nanak called Janam Sakhis, and written in the Punjabi dialect—are filled with myth and stories of miraculous events, invented to justify the semi-deification of the founder of the sect soon after his death. That all the Hindu gods appeared in the sky and announced the birth of a great saint (Bhagat) to save the world, is not quite extraordinary. At an early age he became a diligent student of Vaishnava religious books, and that in his youth he imitated the example of other incipient reformers, wandering to various shrines in search of some clue to the labyrinth of Hinduism. It is even affirmed that his travels included the performance of a hajj to Mecca, and that on being reproved by the Kāzī for lying down with his feet towards the Ka'bah, he replied, 'Put my feet in that direction where the house of God is not.'

Nānak, however, laid no clame to be originator of a new religion. His teaching was mainly founded on that of his predecessors, especially on that of Kabir, whom he constantly quoted. He was simply a Guru, or teacher, and his followers were simply Sikhs or disciples. But he was also a reformer who aimed, as other reformers had done before him at delivering Hinduism, and especially the Vāishṅavism of Northern India, from its incubus of caste, superstition, and idolatry. Yet it does not appear that Nanak directly attacked caste or denounced it in violent language. He simply welcomed persons of all ranks as his followers, and taught that the Supreme Being was no 'respecter or persons.'

The plain fact was that Nanak found himself in a part of India where Muhammadans formed a majority of the population. Though himself originally a Hindu, he denounced idolatry. His idea was to bring about a union between Hindus and Muhammadans on the common ground of a belief in one God. Yet the creed of Nanak was really more pantheistic than monotheistic. God, he said, is Supreme Lord over all (Parameṡvara). He may be called Brāhṁa, or by other names, such as Govinda, etc., but his especial name is Hari (=Vishnu).

This Supreme Being does not create the Universe out of nothing, but evolves it out of himself. It is a kind of expansion of his own essence which takes place for his own amusement (khela) such expansion being made up of the three Gūṇas, Sāttva, Rājas, and Tāmas, in perfect equilibrium. It is Illusion or Māya which disturbes this equilibrium and causes the apparent separation between God, the world, and the human soul. All this is pure Brahmanism. We find also that, except in denouncing idolatry, Nanak differed very little from a pure Vāishṇava, for he taught that in the present age of the world (the Kaliyuga) the repetition of the name of Hari is only means of salvation—not withstanding the merit to be gained by benevolent works and religious ceremonies—and that the knowledge of this name is only to be acquired through a properly ordained teacher (Gūru). It is curious, too, that a religious movement which commenced in an effort to draw the adherents of Sikhism and Islam together, should have ended in exciting the bitterest animosity between the two.

Nanak's death is known to have occurred in October, 1538. One of his sons was expected to succeed him but to the surprise of those who were present at his death, he passed over his own son and nominated as second Gūru his disciple Lahana, whose name had, so to speak, given up his person (aṅga) to the service of his master. This appears to have been his chief merit. He was quite illiterate, though tradition makes him the inventor of the peculiar alphabet called Gūru-mukhi (a modification of the Devaṅgari) in which the Sikh granth was written. Āṅgada nominated Amardas to succed him as third Guru. Seven others were appointed to the succession in a similar manner. These make up the ten chief Gūrus of the Sikh religion. They were, 4. Ramdas; 5. Arjun; 6. Teg-Bahadur; and 10. Govind Singh.

Professor Trumpp has given an interesting account of each, though he does not vouch for the truth of the native biograpohies from which his details are taken. One thing is certain, that notwithstanding the agreement of Sikhs and Muhammadans in regard to the great doctrine of the Unity of the God-head, a violent political antagonism soon sprung up between them. The truth was, that when the Sikhs began to combine together for the promotion of their worldly as well as spiritual interests, they rapidly developed military tastes and abilities. This was the signal for an entire change of attitude between Sikhs and Muhammadans. So long as the former were a mere religious sect they were left unmolested; but when they began to band themselves together for purposes of political aggrendizement, they encountered opposition and persecution. The Muhammadann Government naturally took alarm. It could not permit the growth of an imperium in imperio. Interneceine struggles followed. Both parties treated each other as deadly enemies; but the hardy and energetic Sikhs, though occasionally vanquished and dispered, were not to be driven off the field. Nor is it surprising that they gradually developed a taste for rapine and spoliationl. The decaying Mogul Empire was quite unable to hold its own against their aggressiveness. Ultimately, they combined into powerful association (misals) under marauding chiefs. seized large tracts of land, and took possession of the whole Panjab.

The first to inspire the Sikhs with a desire for political union was the fourth Guru, Ramdās. He was himself a quiet unassuming man, but he understood the value of money and the advantage of organization. His affable manners attacted crowds of adherents, who daily flocked to his house and voluntarily presented him with offerings. With the contributions thus received he was able to purchase the tank called Amritasar (sanskrit Amrita-saras, 'lake of necter'), and build the well-known lake temple which afterwards became a rallying point and centre of union for the whole Sikh community.

Rām dās conveyed his precepts to his followers in the form of verses. Many of his stanzas, together with the sayings of the previous Gurus, and especially of the first

Guru, Nanak, were for the first time collected by his son, the fifth, Guru, Arjun, who was appointed by his father to the Guruship just before his death in 1581. From that time forward the succession was made hereditary and the remaining five Gurus were regarded as rulers rather than as teachers.

With regard to the fifth Guru, Arjun, it may be observed that he was a worthy successor of his father. He perceived that to keep his Sikhs or disciples together, it would be necessary to give them a written standard of authority, and some sort of machinery of government. It is him, therefore, that the Sikhs owe the compilation of their sacred book—called the Granth, or book (Sanskrit Grantha)—and to him is due the establishment of an organized system of collecting a regular tax from all adherents of the sect in different localities. Moreover, under him the sacred tank and temple founded by Ramdās became the nucleus of the sacred town Amritsar, which is still the metropolis of the Sikh religion. He was the first Sikh Pope who aimed at temporal as well as spiritual power. It is not surprising, then, that his death is said to have been brough about by the Emperor Jahangir.

The lives of the sixth, seventh, and eighth Gurus may be passed over as unimportant. The ninth Guru, Teg-Bahadur, attracted the attention of the Emperor Aurangzeb. This fanatical monarch, who was bent on forcing the whole world to embrace Islam, did not long leave the Sikhs undisturbed. He imprisoned Teg Bahadur, and tortured him so cruelly that the Guru, despairing of life, induced a fellow-prisoner to put an end to his sufferings, but Aurangzeb's tyranny was quite powerless to suppress the Sikh movement. It was rather the chief factor in Sikh progress. The murder of the ninth Guru was the great turning-point in the history of the sect. Thenceforward the Sikhs became a nation of fighting men.

Teg Bahadur's son, Govind Singh, succeeded as tenth Gūru. Burning to revenge his father's death, he formed the ambitious design of establishing an independent dominion on the ruins of the Mahammadan Empire. He was a man of extraordinary energy and strength of will, but, born and brought up at Patna, was deeply imbued with Hindu superstitious feelings. He thought better to prepare himself for what he felt was too gigantic a task to be accomplished without supernatural assistance, he went through a course of severe religious austerity. He even so far abjured the principles of his predecessors as to propitiate the Goddess Dūrgā. Nay, it is even afirmed that, instigated by the Brahmans to offer one of his own sons as a sacrifice, and unable to obtain the mother's consent, he allowed one of his disciples to be beheaded as a substitute at the alter of the goddess. The story is noteworthy as pointing to the probable prevalence of humann sacrifice at the time in Upper India.

In fact, it was the tenth Guru, Govind who converted the Sikhs into a nation of fighting men. His character was a curious compounds of pugnacity, courage, superstition, and fanaticism, If Nanak, the first Guru, was the founder of the Sikh religion, Govind, the tenth Guru, was the founder of Sinkh nationality. Many other reformers had attempted to abolish caste as a religious institution, but Govind regarded the evils of caste from a purely political standpoint. He perceived that the power exercised over the Hindus by the Muhammadans and other conquerors was mainly due to the disunion caused by caste. He, therefore, at the risk of offending the most inveterate Hindu prejudices, proclaimed social equality among all the members of this Sikh community.

Nor was this all. He devised other plans for uniting his followers into a distinct people. They were to add the name Singh ('lion') to their names. They were to be distinguished by long hair, they were always to carry a sword in token of engaging in perpetual warfare with the Muslims—to refrain from smoking tobacco, and to wear short pair of trousers, instead of the ordinary Dhotī. They were to be called Khalsa, or the peculiar property of the Guru, and were to be admitted as disciples by a kind of baptismal rite called Pahul that is to say, sugar was dissolved in water, consecrated by the repetition of certain texts taken from the Granth, and stirred with a two-edged sword. They part of this decoction—euphemistically styled nectar—was administered to each new disciple, and the rest sprinkled on the head, mouth, eyes, and other parts of his body, while he was made to take an oath not to mix with certain excommunicated persons, not to worship idols, not to bow to any person whatever, except a Sikh Gūru, and never to turn his back on a foe.

Govind even composed a second sacred book (Granth), which was added as a supplement to the first, and called the book of the tenth Guru. The precepts of Nanak and his successors, which had been compiled by Arjun, were too full of passages suggestive of meekness and pacific feelings. In his own supplement Govind adhered to the religious teaching of the Adi-Granth, but he introduced precepts the direct object of which was to rouse the martial ardour of his followers. He deliberately substituted war for peace as a religious duty. Thenceforward they were to imitate the Muhammadans—they were to spread their religion, not by persuasion, but by fire and sword. Nay, more, they were to live by the sword, and even to worship the sword.

Govind was himself more of a military than a religious leader. He was not only a brave soldier, but a daring and resolute commander, and his fighting propensities were intensified by his innate superstition and fanaticism.

It need not, therefore, be matter of astonishment that the greater part of Govind's own life was passed in strife and warfare. But he was no match for the Emperor Aurangzeb, who was his equal in fanatical intolerance, and greatly his superior in ability and military resources. He retired to Central India and built himself a large residence in Malwa (called Damdama). This place is still a central point of resort for the Sikh community. On the death of Aurangzeb, Govind is said to have gained the goodwill of military command in the Dekhan. There a certain Pathan, who owed him a grudge, attempted his assassination and wounded him severely. He is said to have lingered some time, but eventually died of his injuries at a town called Nader, in the valley of the Godavari (A.D. 1707).

Perhaps the most remarkable feature of the later Sikh system was the quasi-deification of the sacred book, or Granth. Govind refused to appoint a successor to the Guruship, but he well knew that to maintain the Sikh religion as a distinctive creed some visible representative and standard of authority was needed. He therefore consitituted the Granth a kind of permanent religious Guru, gifting it with personality, and even endowing it with the personal title *Sahib* (Lord). 'After me,' he said, 'you shall everywhere mind the book of the Granth-Sahib as your Guru; whatever you shall ask it will show you.'

I select a few examples from different parts of the book, slightly abridged and altered from Professor Trumpp's version:—

At the beginning is True One.

The True One is, O Nanak ! and the True One also will be.

Know, that there are two ways (that of Hindus and that of Nusalmans), but only one Lord.

By thyself all the creation is produced; by thyself, baving created, the whole is caused to disappear.

Thou, O Hari, alone art inside and outside; thou knowest the sacrets (of the heart).

Müller the name of Hari, Hari, O my heart, by which comfort is brought about; by which all sins and vices disappear; by which poverty and pain cease.

Thou art I, I an thou, or what kind is the difference ? Like gold and the bracelet like water and wave.

In the seven insular continents, the seven oceans, the nine regious the four Vedas, teh eighteen Puranas: in all, thou, O Hari, art abiding; in all thy decree, O Hari, iss working.

By the perfect Guru the name of Hari is made firm in me. Hari is my beloved, my king. If some one bring and unite (him with me), my life is revived.

Thou art my father, my mother, my cousin, my brother, my protector in all places. Then what fear and grife can there be to me ? By thy mercy I have known thee. Thou art my support, my trust. Without thee there is none other; all is they play and thy arena, O Lord !

The Lord is my dear friend. He is sweeter to me than mother and father, sister, brother, and all friends; like thee there is none other, O Lord !

Be united with the Lord of the Universe. After a long time this (human) body was obtained. In some births thou wast made a rock and mountain. In some births thou wast produced as a pot-herb. In the eighty -four lakhs (of forma fo existence) thou wast caused to wander about.

No hot wind touches those who are protecled by the true Guru. The Guru is the true creator.

Protected by the Guru he is admitted to the tru house and palace (of Hari). Death cannot eat him.

I am continually a sartifice tomy my own Guru.

I am become a sacrifice to my own Lord. From the Veda, from the book (the Kuran), from the whole world he is conspicuous. The king of Nanak is openly seen.

Having forgotten all things mediate on the One ! Drop false conceit, offer up (they) mind and body !

The following are examples of Kabir's sayings quoted in the Granth:—

Kabir says: I am the worst of all, every one is good except me.
Death, of which the world is afraid, is joy to my mind.
The gate of salvation is narrow, not wider than the tenth Part of a mustard seed.
If I make the seven oceans link, if I make the trees my pen, if I make the earth my paper, the glory of God (Hari) cannot be written.
Hope should be placed on God (Ram), hope in others in useless.
What thou art doing to morrow do now' what thou art doing now do at once. Afterwards nothing will be done when death descends on the head.

It wiil be sufficiently evident from these passage that Sikhism was a great religious reform, and yet in its essence very little better than either Vāishṇavism or Brāhmanism. The Granth declares the One sess of the Deity, but when we sound the depths of its inner doctrines we find that this unity is based on substratumm of pantheistic ideas, There is but One God, but He manifests Himself everywhere and is every thing. From various passages of the Granṭh it is clear that the Vaishnava names Hari, Kṛiṣhṇa, Rama, and Govinda are accepted by the Sikhs as names of the Supreme. They are even willing to regard the different divine personalities represented by these names as manifestations of the one Supreme Being. The point on which they pride themselves is the prohibition of image-worship. Yet they make an ido of their own sacred book, worshipping it as truly as the Hindus do their idols, dressing it, decorating it, fanning it putting it to bed at night, and treating it much in the same manner as the idols of Kṛiṣhṇa are treated.

We have seen that one great distinguishing feature of their system is that war is made an essetial part of religion. To indicate their belief in this doctrine they woeship the military weapons of their Gūrus. In other respects they conform to the customs of the Hindus. They even surpass the ordinary Hindu insome of his most inveterate superstitions; as, for exmple, inascribing divine sanctity to the cow. The killing of a cow is with Sikhs, the most heinous of crimes, meriting nothing less than capital punishment not, however, from any infuction to that effect in the Graṇth, but from simple opposition to the Musalmans, who, whenever they conquered any distict peopled by Hindus, invariably slaughtered cows, both to ratify their victories and to show their contemps for Hindu superstitions.

That again they accept in all its fulness the HIndu doctrine of metempsychosis, believing, that there are eighty-four lakhs (or eight million four hundred thousand) of forms of existence through which the soul—represented as flames emanating from the great fountain of life are liable to pass before returning to their source. These forms of life are supposed to consist of 2,300,000 quadrupeds; 1,100,000 creeping animals; 1,700,000 immovable creatures (such as trees and stones); 1,400,000 forms of human beings. Final emancipation can only be achieved in this last form of existence.

As to the golden temple at Amritsar, called Hari-mandira, 'the temple of Hari,' or sometimes Durbar Sahib, it may be said to rank next to the Taj at Agra as one of the most striking sights of India. To form an idea of a unique spectacle presented by this sacred locality, one must picture to oneself a large square sheet of water, bordered by a marble pavement, in the centre of a picturesque Indian town. Around the margin of this artificial lake are clustered numerous fine mansions, most of them once the property of Sinkh chiefs who assembled here every year, and spent vast sums on the endowment of the central shrine. One of the houses was occupied by Sirdar Mangal Singh Ramgharia, a well known and much esteemed member which enjoyed a grand panoramic view of the lake and it vicinity—one of those rare sights seen at intervals during life, which fix themselves indelibly on the memory. In the centre of the water rises the beautiful temple with its gilded dome and cupolas, approached by a marble causeway. It is quite unlike any other place of worship to be seen throughout India, and in structure and appearance may be regarded as a kind of compromise between a Hindu temple and Muhammadan mosque, reminding one of the attempted compromise between Hinduism and Islam, which was once a favourite idea with both Kabīr and Nānak.

Although the temple is free from images, and is dedecated to the one God under his name Hari (applied also to Kriṣhṇa or Vishṇu), a visible representation of invisible God is believed to be present in sacred book. The Granth is, in fact, the real divintiy of the shrine, and is treated as if it had a veritable personal existence. Every morning it is dressed out in costly brocade, and reverently placed on a low throne under a jewelled conopy, said to have been constructed by Ranjit Singh at a cost of 50,000 rupees. All day long chowries are waved over the sacred volume, and every evening it is transported to the second temple on the edge of the lake opposite the causeway, where it is made to repose for the night in a golden bed within consecrated chamber, railed off and protected from all profane intrusion by bolts and bars.

But Sikhism was not the only offshoot of the school founded by the great reformer Kabīr. He is said to have twelve disciples, like his predecessor Rāmānand; and each disciple is supposed to have taken a distinct line (paṅtha) of his own, and to have originated a distinct school of religious thought.

Two of these may be singled out for special notice—the Dādu-paṅthis, and the Satnamīs.

The Dādu-paṅthis, as their name implies, were founded

by Dādu, a cotton-cleaner of Ahmadābād, who flourished about A.D. 1600. They are really Vāishṇava Theists like the Sikhs; that is, worshippers of the one God under one of the names of Viṣhṇu, according to the doctrine of Kabir, on whose precepts the religious works of the sect are all founded.

In the same way the Satnāmis are only Vāishṇava Theists, who call the one God by a peculiar name of their own (Satnām), and base their doctrines like the Sikhs on Kabir's school of theology.

According to Professor H.H. Wilson, the founder of the Satnāmis was Jagjivandās, a native of Oudh, whose *samadh* or tomb is shown at Katwa, a place between Lucknow and Ayodhya. He is said to have flourished about the year 1750, and to have written certain tracts in Hindi, called Jñānaprakasa, Maha-pralaya, and Prathama-granṭha. There is also a branch of Satnāmis who are followers of a low caste Chamār named Ghasidas and his son Balak-dās, who flourished about the beginning or this century. I was able to obtain some account of their tenets and practices from the missionaries of the Church Missionary Society at Madras. They are also described in one or two numbers of the Madras Missionary Record for 1872.

Like other varieties of Hindu Unitarians, all of whom mix up pantheistic ideas with monotheistic doctrines, they submit implicitly to their Gurus, regarding them as viceregents of God upon earth, and occasionally as actual incarnations of the Deity.

The following are a few of cheif precepts and rules:—

> God pervades the universe. He is present in every single thing. The title Lord (Sāhib) should be added to every object in which God is present. God is the spring and source of everything good and evil. Idols must not be worshipped. The ordained religious teacher (Guru) is holy. Even the water in which his feet are washed is

holy, and should be drunk by his disciples. Distinctions of caste are not to be observed. Fasts need not be kept. Feed the poor. Wound no one's feelings. When the dead are burnt let no one cry or weep; let them only exclaim, 'The Lord gave, and the Lord has taken away !'

Foot Notes:

1. So the naṁe was interpreted to me, but I suspect it properly meaṅs 'fight quitter, and rather refers to Kriṣhṇa's declinine to take part in the great war of the Māhābhārata, between the sons of Pāṅdu and Dhritārāshtrā.
2. The text has been edited with a translation, and is published in jounral of the Royal Asiatic Society of October 1882.
3. It is a characteristic of the Svami-Narayana sect that pictures, instead of images, are used in some of their temples.
4. Of these only six are now generally performed, *viz.*:—(1) the birth ceremany, or touching the tongue of a new born infant with clarified butter, etc.; (2) the name-giving ceremony on the tenth day' (3) tonsure; (4) induction into the privileges of the twice-born by investiture with the sacred thread; (5) solemn return home from the house of a preceptor after completing the prescribed course of study; (6) marriage. They will be described in a subsequent chapter.
5. The six daily duties (called Nityakarman) according to Parasara are:—(1) bathing; (2) morning and evening prayer (saṅdhya); (3) offerings to fire (hoṁa); (4) repetition of the Vedā; (5) worship of ancestors; (6) worship of gods.
6. Selected from H.H. Wilson's *Hindu Religious Sects*.
7. Professor Trumpp designates it by this name. I believe I was one of the first to recomend its being so distinguished, in the preface to the first edition of my *Sanskrit-English Dictionary*, published by the University of Oxford in 1872.
8. At one time in the Punjab it was infinitely more criminal to kill a cow than to kill a daughter.

Three

SRIVAISNAVISM AND THE TIRUMALA LORD

1) Indispensability of Religion

Man, as a spiritual being cannot lead his life in peace and happiness without the support of religion. He instinctively clutches hold of the hands of a superior power in times of stress and distress when he knows that the situation he faces is hopeless and totally beyond his control. Religion is the very foundation on which the SANATANA DHARMA or the eternal way of life is based. In fact, religion has been the guiding spirit of Vedic religion and culture. Belief in God is the very core of the spiritual way of life. Mahatma Gandhi succinctly gives expression to this truth with the words "Remove God from my life and I am dead."

2) Satyasya Satyam—The Ultimate in Truth

The eternal and the ephemeral exist in the world side by side and the Vedic seers were the first to find out the eternal truths in regard to the singleness of Godhead, the immortality of the soul, the unity of all existence and the divinity of man. Their quest for truth began outwards with the external world, turned inwards towards the mind and moved upwards to know the Satyasya Satyam or the ultimate in truth and reality. They pondered over the fundamental problems of human life and discovered that at the substratum of all existence and realities, there is one Primeval Being and all the realities of the physical universe are only His manifestations. Both Srutis (Vedas) and the Smritis (Itihasas or epics, Puranas or ancient historical accounts, Dharma-shastras or Code of Ethics and the Agamas or manual of worship proclaim this *Satyasya Satyam* or the ultimate truth. of spiritual unity behind the physical diversity. In the various Vedic passages, the self same single truth with the words PURUSHA EVADAGUM SARVAM i.e.Purusha is all this, ISAVASYAM IDAGUM SARVAM, *i.e.*, "all this is pervaded by the Lord", SARVAM KHALVIDAM BRAHMA, "Brahman (The Creator) is all this", VASUDEVA SARVAM, "all this is Vasudeva", SARVAM VISHNUMAYAM JAGAT, "that the entire universe is Supreme Lord Vishnu is widely proclaimed".

What the contemporary world badly needs today is the spiritual wisdom or *Satyasya Satyam* of Vedanta so essential to transform the human outlook from bestiality to divinity. This spiritual message can only help to replace selfishness, greed, hatred, envy, and violence by love, compassion, justice, equity, truth, peace, happiness and freedom. Man cannot live in peace either with himself or with the world without understanding the purpose of human life and the meaning of the inevitable death. There are only two ways of finding out the basic truths of life in the mundane world. One way is to find it out for oneself through the very difficult and never ending path of trial and error and the other is to rely on the verbal testimony of the trustworthy and reliable seers who have left behind for the benefit of posterity the highest in human and divine wisdom. As it will be humanly impossible for any one to find the *Satyasya Satyam* or the ultimate in truth within one life time through self-efforts, it will be safe and wise to rely wholly on the Vedas, which as a solicitous mother, provide the clearest and best account of the ultimate truth and reality.

3) Enternal Message of Vedanta

Vedanta is the culmination of the Vedas being their end portion containing a summary of the final conclusions of the Vedas. The end portion of the Vedas contains the Upanishads or the esoteric teachings. The essence of the Vedas is contained in the Upanishads, which are the most closely guarded secrets revealed only to the deserving. The sublime truths contained in the Upanishads are the very summit of the Vedic philosophical knowledge and spiritual wisdom. The Upanishads are, therefore, considered supremely important as the truths revealed by them are believed to be the most authoritative, eternal, infallible and universally valid. The word UPANISHAD means esoteric teachings, which are hidden or concealed in the various passages and so not readily apparent. These truths are, therefore, imparted by a competent teacher only to the deserving disciples who can comprehend them.

Fearing that the esoteric teachings contained in the Srutis (Vedas revealed or heard) which have come down through the ages in Karna Parampara, or oral transmission, over hundreds of generations should not be lost to posterity, there have been supplementary texts called Smritis (*i.e.* what is remembered) to preserve the highest truths contained in the Vedas. The two Itihasas or epics (*i.e.* truths as they are) namely Ramayana and Mahabharata and the Sattvika (wise) Puranas or ancient historical accounts have attempted to communicate the highest truths of the Vedas in simple story form for the benefit of lay people. The most salutary principle to be strictly adhered to in the acceptance of the truths remembered or recapitulated in the Smritis or the supplementary texts is that they should be fully in accord with the Srutis or the divine revelations contained in the Vedas. The epic Mahabharatha contains the world renowned Srimad Bhagavad Gita, or the Song Celestial, which is considered as the very essence of the Upanishads. In fact, the Gita is included as one of the three authoritative scriptural texts of Vedanta. The philosophy of the Upanishads has been encoded in terse aphoristic form in another supplementary text called the Brahma Sutras, or the Vedanta Sutras, authored by a sage named Badarayana. The Brahma Sutras are also called Uttara Mimamsa or Sariraka Mimamsa.

The philosophical system of Vedanta is based on three scriptural texts collectively called the Prasthana Traya or scriptural trinity comprising the Upanishads, Srimad Bhagavad Gita and the Vedanta Sutras. All the schools of Vedanta philosophy, which came in the medieval age, are based on the scriptural trinity only.

4) Central Teaching of the Upanishads

Traditionally it is believed that there are 108 Upanishads, which contain the mystic experiences of various seers at different times. Of these, a dozen called the major or the principal Upanishads are counted as the most authoritative being the oldest of all the Upanishads. All the schools of Vedanta philosophy agree that the main teaching of the Upanishads is enshrined in the declaration EKAMEVA ADVITIYAM: "One only without a second". However, there is no agreement even amongst the best of the intellectuals as to what the Upanishads exactly mean in the cryptic declaration of One only. Is it Monotheism (One God with personal form) or Pantheism (God is everything) or Absolutism (Impersonal formless God) or Monism (Immanent All-pervasive God) or Dualism (Independent God with dependent entities)or a combination of any or all these concepts.

Modern intellectuals who have not understood the esoteric purport of the mystic truths intuited by the Vedic seers naively conclude that the Upanishads do not present any coherent and consistent system of philosophy and are an odd assortment of diverse ideas which are mutually conflicting and contradictory. An in-depth study and careful analysis of the Upanishads reveal two definite approaches to the concept of Brahman (Creator). Of the principal Upanishads, the ones like Isavasya, Katha, Mundaka, Prasna and beginning portions of Chandogya Upanishad are positively Monotheistic propounding a Brahman with form and attributes. Certain other Upanishads like the Mandukya, Aittiriya and Brihadaranyaka are patently Absolutistic, Pantheistic and Monistic describing the all-pervasive Brahman as formless and attributeless.

The major Upanishads believed to be the oldest have not appeared simultaneously but at different periods of time. In the absence of some knowledge about the chronology of the principal Upanishads, it is very difficult to conclude, only on the basis of the archaic language or the contents of these Upanishads, whether the Monotheistic Upanishads appeared first or the Absolutistic ones. The Upanishads are neither pure philosophy nor pure religion but a fine blend of both. Philosophy is only a support of religion and does not have an independent existence of its own. Philosophy lays the intellectual foundation for the practice of religion with conviction and faith. The Absolutism of philosophy is only for the intellectuals and is of little relevance for the common man who goes only by faith.

The fundamental doctrines contained in the Upanishads seem to have had their origin in the Samhitas of the Rig-Veda which are believed to be the most ancient in point of time. Researchers who have carried out a thorough study of the Rig Veda are of the considered view that the Purusha Sukta, Nasadiya Sukta and the hymn to the unknown God, which find a place in the Tenth and the last Mandala (Section) of the Rig Veda may possibly be the earliest and perhaps the most ancient. These experts opine that the origin of the thought of Oneness of Godhead could directly be traced to these three hymns of the Rig-Veda. Some intellectuals, therefore, conclude that the concept of Brahman as an impersonal, unmanifest Absolute Reality found in some Upanishads could have emanated from the Nasadiya Sukta and/or the hymn to the unknown God. Similarly the perception of the Creator as a person with auspicious attributes described in the theistic Upanishads could have originated from the Purusha Sukta hymn.

There appears to be considerable force and some element of truth in this conclusion of intellectuals as the Supreme Lord Himself in His incarnation as Sri Krishna, in verse 3 of Chapter III of the Gita says: "O Arjuna, in this world, two courses of disciplines have been communicated by Me, in the ancient past; that of Sankhya with the path of knowledge and that of Karma Yoga along the path of selfless work." From the colophon at the end of each chapter of Gita, it is observed that in the dialogue between Sri Krishna and Arjuna, the Supreme Lord taught the science of Brahman contained in the Upanishads and the Yoga scriptures. Theistic Upanishads like the Katha and Mundaka refer to the doctrine of Grace for knowing Brahman and they specifically advocate meditation (Yoga) as the most efficacious means to realize Brahman. Both the theistic and the absolutistic Upanishads based on the Purusha and the Nasadiya Suktas (hymns) respectively of the Rig-Veda have emanated from the BREATH OF THE ETERNAL which is perhaps referred to by the Lord in the Gita. The Vedas are called the Nigama while the God-oriented selfless actions of worship are covered by the term Agama.

5) Genesis of the Nigama and the Agama Traditions

The Vedas are broadly divided into two parts namely the Karma Kanda and the Jnana Kanda. The ritualistic portion which forms the bulk of the scripture comprising the Samhitas (hymns), Brahmanas (sacrifices) and Aranyakas (inner significance of hymns and sacrifices) comes under the Karma Kanda. The Jnana Kanda or knowledge portion refers to the philosophic concepts contained in the various Upanishads. The philosophy of the Upanishads, which seek the eternal has been the logical outcome of the ritualistic practices which aimed at the temporal and the ephemeral. In this sense the Vedas form a comprehensive, consistent and undivided whole and the division into two parts has been only to understand the broad contents.

Ancient Vedic civilization seems to have adopted two main streams of religious tradition viz. the Nigama tradition of fire sacrifices and the Agama tradition of image worship. The Vedas, which are otherwise known as Nigama, advocate the performance of sacrifices in consecrated fire to propitiate the different gods. These sacrifices are detailed in the Karma Kanda or the ritualistic portion of the Vedas. The practice of worship (Upasana) and meditation (Yoga) are described in the Jnana Kanda or knowledge portion. Knowledge without action has no practical relevance while actions without knowledge can lead to dangerous consequences. The Nigama or Vedic sacrifices and the Agama or worship (Upasana) of consecrated images form the bedrock of ancient tradition on which the religion of the Vedas seems to have been based. The term "Agama" means sacred declarations that have come down from the Divine while the word "Nigama" also means revelations that have emanated from the Divine.

The followers of Agama tradition, while accepting the Vedas (Nigama) as Divine revelations of knowledge of realities, follow the practices of worship prescribed in the Agama, which is revered by them as Srutis or what has been divinely ordained. The origin of the Agama tradition is traced to the Vedas. In fact, Dr. S.N.Dasgupta in his monumental work entitled *The History of Indian Philosophy* holds the view that the Agama doctrines could be associated with the Purusha Sukhta of the Rig-Veda and the Satapatha Brahmana of the Yajur Veda. So the origin of the Agama tradition which is traced to the Vedas by its followers seems to be fundamentally sound as it is based on proper scriptural testimony.

Nigama and Agama are the two eyes of the ancient Vedic religion. It is really very unfortunate that the extent of attention paid to the preservation of the Nigama tradition has not been bestowed on the Agama tradition. The Agama tradition seems to have receded into the background during the post-Vedic period till the period of Mahabharatha. There is thus a crucial gap in the proper understanding of the

Agama tradition because of absence of ancient texts particularly between the period of Sathapata Brahmana and the Narayaniya section of the Mahabharatha, which makes specific reference to the Agama doctrines. During the period of the Puranas, charges seem to have been leveled against the Agama tradition saying that its fundamental tenets were anti-Vedic, by some upper caste people who did not probably know the Vedic origin of the tradition. Yamunacharya (Alavandar), a Sri Vaishnavite Acharya who preceded Sri Ramanuja, very competently refuted these charges in his treatise called AGAMA PRAMANYAM, which seems to have paved the way for the revival of the ancient Agama tradition.

6) **Vedic Origin of Vaishnavism**

Vaishnavism or the monotheistic worship of Lord Vishnu as the Supreme God of all the Vedic gods seems to have been the prevalent religion from very ancient times and this religion is wholly of Vedic origin. The Supreme Lord Himself is the progenitor of the Vedas, which are His Breath Eternal. The Vedas describe only His glory and greatness. Unquestionable evidence in support of the fact that Vaishnavism has had its roots in the Vedas is found in the hymns of the Vedas themselves. It can, therefore, be said with reasonable degree of certainty that the origin of Vaishnavism can be traced to the dim dawn of Rig Vedic civilization when the Nigama and Agama traditions seem to have existed side by side. This is quite understandable as many must have opted for the Agama worship as they must have found the Nigama sacrifices too difficult to follow both in letter and spirit.

In the pre-historic times, the Vedas were verbally recited and the written form came into existence only after the discovery of script. The Vedas have come down to posterity through oral transmission over hundreds of generations and none knows for certain the beginning of the Vedas. It is quite possible that the arrangement of the ancient hymns must have undergone changes over the millennia. It is, therefore, virtually impossible to determine with any degree of accuracy which were the earliest hymns and which were the later ones only on the basis of the language of the hymns. Without knowing the proper sequence and the chronology of the divine revelations, any conclusion in regard to the purport of Vedas based on the passages of the Vedas in its extant form can only be erroneous and inaccurate. The Vedas are APAURUSHEYA *i.e.* of Divine origin and so dating them or knowing the exact order in which the revelations were received is far beyond the ingenuity of the human intellect. The history of the ancient Vedic civilization as recorded by the Western intellectuals with their Biblical background without understanding the ground realities of the Orient cannot, therefore, be considered either reliable or trustworthy.

7) Ultimate Truth of the Vedas

Vedas are the timeless heritage of entire mankind as they are the earliest religious literature available to humanity. The order followed in the existing arrangement of the Vedic hymns cannot be considered as the sole criterion to fix the sequence of the hymns as they are not human compositions. The status and importance of the various gods in the hierarchy of the Vedic pantheon cannot be decided by going through the individual passages in the Vedas. What the Vedic seers originally envisaged is far more important than the superficial conclusion on the basis of the letter of the Vedas. Therefore, there appears to be no justification or need to undertake an elaborate exercise of finding out the number of references to various gods in the different passages of the Vedas to decide conclusively the place of importance of a particular deity among the various gods.

Vedas declare the glory and greatness of the Creator and His various creations. In order to know who is the Creator so as to distinguish Him from all His creations, it will be necessary to take an integrated and comprehensive view of the inner purport of the Vedas as a whole, keeping in view the contents of the Smiritis also *i.e.* the supplementary scriptures like the Itihasas and the Satwika Puranas. Vedas, which run to thousands of hymns, is a veritable maze and to find a way out of it to decide the Supreme God who is the author of the physical universe will need a proper understanding of all realities. The Gita puts the problem in a nutshell with the words "As much use as there is of a reservoir in a place flooded from all sides with water, so much there is of all the Vedas for a Brahmin who knows."

Saintly souls who have thoroughly understood the esoteric purport of the Vedas have already done the elaborate exercise of going through the entire Vedas to know the Ultimate Truth contained in them. For the benefit of posterity they have declared their unanimous conclusion with the words *VEDESU PAURUSHAM SUKHTAM*, *i.e.*, "among the Vedas, the Purusha Sukhta is the most important as this hymn contains the very essence of the Vedas." This seems to be the reason why this hymn is placed in the last Mandala or the concluding Section of the Rig-Veda. The truth declared by the saintly souls is substantiated by the fact that the hymn describing the creation of the universe by the Cosmic Being is perhaps the one and only hymn of its kind which finds a place in all the four Vedas. In fact, the Moksha Dharma section in the great epic Mahabharatha which is designated as the FIFTH VEDA declares: "The Purusha is extolled in all the Vedas as He is the very essence of these Vedas." The central truth of all the Vedas is that the Supreme Purusha as the Creator of the universe is the Ultimate Truth.

Who is this Purusha? The answer to this question is provided by the Katha Upanishad, which says that there is nothing higher than the Purusha. And the highest goal of human life has been declared as VISHNOR YAD PARAMAM PADAM *i.e.* the highest abode of Lord Vishnu. Suffice it to say that the Brahman or the Creator is the Purusha of the Purusha Sukhta and Lord Vishnu of the Vedas as also the Katha Upanishad.

The three giant strides made by Lord Vishnu covering the terrestrial, celestial and the cosmic regions, His all pervasive nature as the inner ruler of all His creations, His Highest Abode called the Parama Pada or the Kingdom of Immortality, His ability to take various Avataras or incarnations as fish, tortoise, boar, dwarf etc, which are detailed in the various passages of the Vedas single Him out as the Ultimate Truth of the Vedas. He is the Supreme Being, God of Vedic gods, One without a second, and the Creator of all. In fact, only the Creator can take incarnations and not any of His creations and only He can be the Lord of Immortality to allow entry of His creations into His Parama Pada. Lord Vishnu is, therefore, the central and ultimate truth of all the Vedas which extol only His glory and greatness. All the supplementary scriptural texts like the Itihasas, Puranas etc reiterate the same truth of the Vedas.

Sri Ramanuja derives the word 'BRAHMAN' from the Sanskrit root BRIH, which means great. He concludes that the Upanishadic term Brahman means the Greatest, Highest and the most Supreme in every respect. Based on the testimony of the Prasthana Thraya the scriptural trinity and keeping in view the clarifications in the Smritis or supplementary scriptural texts, Sri Ramanuja has very ably concluded that Brahman the ultimate truth of the Vedas refer only to Lord Vishnu who is also called Narayana and Vasudeva by the Vedas themselves. He has competently proved without any shadow of doubt on the basis of scriptural testimony that the Vedas preach only Saguna Upasana of Eka Devatha *i.e.* monotheistic worship of the one Supreme Lord Vishnu without a second with bewitching personality of His own and endowed with unsurpassable auspicious attributes totally devoid of blemishes.

The greatest declaration in the oldest Rig Veda is EKAM SAT, VIPRA BAHUDA VADANTI *i.e.*Ultimate Reality is One only; the wise describe It in many ways. The very same truth is echoed by the Upanishads with the words EKAMEVE

ADVITIYAM *i.e.* One only without a second. Eminent sages have elaborated and clarified this single truth with the words SARVA DEVA NAMASKARAM KESAVAM PRATIGACCHATI *i.e.* the salutations offered to the various gods of the Vedic pantheon ultimately reach the Supreme Lord Kesava alone. This clarification reminds one of the passage in the Mahabharatha which says VEDASHASTRAM PARAM NASTI NA DAIVAM KESAVAT PARAM *i.e.* there is no scripture higher than the Vedas and there is no God greater than Kesava. This fact has been reiterated by Lord Krishna Himself in verse 23 of Chapter IX of Bhagvad Gita where He says "Even those who worship other deities with faith in their heart worship Me alone O Arjuna, though with a mistaken approach."

Vedanta, which reveals the Ultimate Truth, is unfortunately reduced by the Western intellect to a few simple beliefs like formless Brahman, Maya, Avidya, renunciation of the world, practice of other worldly asceticism etc. These people have a very superficial acquaintance with the profound truths of the Vedic religion and philosophy. Vedic religion is strictly monotheistic with One Brahman only as the Supreme Lord and it was Sri Ramanuja who was solely responsible for the revival of the Vedic Vaishnavism.

8) Contribution of Sri Ramanuja to the Revival of Vedic Vaishnavism

Eternal credit goes to Sri Ramanuja who spent a lifetime for the cause of Sri Vaishnavism against very heavy odds. Either on account of vandalism or due to deliberate, pre-meditated and wanton destruction of works in the form of glosses, by insane people belonging to rival faiths who disagreed with the doctrines enunciated in such works or due to the sheer neglect and careless indifference of the followers, several important manuscripts relating to theistic Vedanta recorded during the Epic and Purana periods seem to have irretrievably been lost to posterity. For example, Sage Bodhayana is reported to have recorded very detailed glosses both on

Gita and the Brahma Sutras. This work seems to have been condensed by some of his followers or disciples. This is quite evident from the opening passage of Sri Ramnuja's Sri Bhasya which reads as follows: "The lengthy explanation (Vritti) on the Brahma Sutras which was composed by the revered sage Bodhayana has been abridged by former teachers; according to their views, the words of the Brahma Sutras will be explained in this present work."

Neither the detailed work of the sage Bodhayana nor the summarized versions of his followers like Tanka, Dramida, Guhadeva, Bharuchi, and Kapardin etc.are currently extant. From the biography of Sri Ramanuja it is learnt that the saint traveled by foot all the way from Srirangam in Tamil Nadu to Srinagar in Kashmir to get hold of the only available moth-eaten palm leaf manuscript of the detailed commentary of sage Bodhayana on the Vedanta Sutras of Badarayana. It is very distressing to note that even before Sri Ramanuja could complete his study of the commentary, the manuscript was snatched away from his hands by the followers of the rival faiths who seem to have feared that any writing on the basis of the commentary may disturb the faith of people who believed in the philosophical tenets of the rival faiths. But thanks to the prodigious memory of his disciple named Kuresa who went along with Sri Ramanuja to Srinagar, posterity has been blessed with at least some idea of the profound philosophical wisdom of the ancient sages who strictly adhered to the theistic Vedanta in general and Vaishnavism in particular.

Sri Ramanuja has laid firm philosophical foundation for the worship of Lord Vishnu as the One Supreme Lord of the Vedic Vaishnavism. by propounding the philosophy of Visishtadwaita or PAN-ORGANISMAL MONOTHEISM. All the subsequent Acharyas who came after him like Madhva, Nimbarka, Vallabha, Chaitanya, Svami Narayana, etc., have accepted only the theistic Vedanta and have wholly rejected Absolutism as inconsistent with the philosophy of Vedanta.

Humanity, therefore, owes a deep debt of gratitude to the great savant Sri Ramanuja who in the face of heavy odds and risk to his very life, gave to posterity the pristine Vedic religion of Sri Vaishnavism.

For the practice of religion, the heart of man longs for God with supremely beautiful personal form whom he can see, know, commune, love, pray, prostrate, worship and surrender heart and soul. Sri Ramanuja the great psychologist brought all the intellectual philosophy of the Upanishads close to the heart of common people in the shape of Sri Vaishnavism through the fine blend of the Nigama and the Agama traditions. Through his magnum opus Sri Bhashya, which is his detailed commentary on the Vedanta Sutras and Vedartha Samgraha Sri Ramanuja has very ably proved that Vaishnavism is the one and only religion of the Vedas. He has also established with scriptural testimony that Sri Vaishnavism is based both on the Sruti (Vedas) and the Smritis (supplementary scriptures). In his interpretation of the Vedanta Sutras Sri Ramanuja has admirably combined the philosophy of the Upanishads with the religion of the Vedas by the proper integration of the apparently contradictory passages of the Upanishads with those of the supplementary scriptural texts to bring out the coherence and consistency of all the scriptural texts. He has ably demonstrated that Vedanta is a comprehensive whole and not a jumbled assortment of contradictory ideas and that there is absolutely no inconsistency or conflict in any of the Divine revelations. Philosophy being speculative calls for intellectual acumen whereas religion being based on emotion calls for faith and conviction. Sri Ramanuja has adeptly proved that mere theory without practice can be only lame as it can serve no useful purpose whereas practice without theory can turn out to be blind without any sort of intellectual conviction. That is the very reason why Vedanta combines religion with philosophy.

Sri Ramanuja has authoritatively established with the help of Srutis (Vedas) and Smritis(supplementary scriptural texts) that Brahman of the Upanishads is not a featureless, formless non-entity but a superbly enchanting personality with all unsurpassable auspicious attributes free from imperfections. It is highly unfortunate that the theistic Vedanta propounded by Sri Ramanuja in his philosophy of Visishtadwaita has not gained wide popularity and recognition both within India and abroad. In fact, the study of this philosophy has so far remained only superficial and peripheral and not deep and thorough. It is time that this philosophy, which is fully in accord with the letter and spirit of the Prasthana Traya (scriptural trinity) of Vedanta, receives the due attention that it rightly and richly deserves for a better understanding of the fundamental tenets of Vedic Vaishnavism.

9) Mind of Badarayana, Author of Vedanta Sutras

Did Sage Badarayana who wrote the Vedanta Sutras favour Monotheism (Brahman with form) or Absolutism (Impersonal Brahman)?. What was the system advocated by him as the philosophy of the Upanishads? A very careful and impartial analysis of the Vedanta Sutras reveals that the basic aim of the author of the Vedanta Sutras seems to have been that he desired to prove the authoritative character of the Pancharatra docrines by refuting all the other schools of philosophical thought. In the Second Pada (Part) of the Vedanta Sutras he refutes the claims of both the Vaidic schools like Samkya, Nyaya, Vaiseshika, Yoga and Purva Mimamsa and the non-Vaidic like Bouddha, Jaina, Pasupata etc and takes up the discussion of Pancharatras as the last topic. The author Badarayana seems to have personally favoured theistic Vedanta. In fact, his intention in compiling the Vedanta Sutras seems to have been to prove that the Upanishads as the natural culmination of the Vedas, present a very coherent and consistent religion of Monotheism only and not Absolutism or Pantheism or Monism.

The very name Sariraka Mimamsa given to the Vedanta Sutras seems to covertly indicate the duality in the body-soul relationship between human soul (jivatma) and the Supreme Soul (Paramatma). Some of the major or principal Upanishads seems to manifestly uphold the doctrines of Vaishnaivsm. For example, the Katha Upanishad declares that the journey of the human soul should end in VISHNOR YAD PARAMAM PADAM. The central message of Srimad Bhagawad Gita, which many believe to be anterior to the Brahma Sutras and is one of the scriptural trinity *i.e.* Prasthana Thraya , seems to favour the monotheistic doctrine of the Pancharatra school.

The very fact that sage Badarayana, the author of the Brahma Sutras found it necessary to devote one whole Adhikarana or topic for philosophical discussion called the UTPATYASAMBHAVADHIKARANA exclusively to study the Pancharatra school indicates that in his time this system of philosophical thought must have gained considerable ground as a force to be reckoned with. The Vishnu temples in several places in both the North and the South India seem to have been in existence much before the Christian era, as is evident from the inscriptions at Besnagar and Ghoshundi belonging to the 2nd and the First century respectively. From the time of Mahabharata the worship of Vasudeva as the Supreme Lord seems to have been widely in vogue.

In his interpretation of the four aphorisms in the UTPATYASAMBHAVADIKARANA Sri Ramanuja has firmly established that the Pancharatra doctrines are wholly in accord with the Vedas as the Vyuha forms of Vasudeava are only His incarnations and the eternity of the soul is no where rejected by the Pancharatra school. Sri Ramanuja is, therefore, of the considered view that Sage Badarayana , the author of the Vedanta Sutras is in favour of the Panchartra school of thought as its doctrines are not contradictory to Vedic revelations as the earlier Vaidic and Non-Vaidic schools of philosophy. In Sri Ramanuja's view this Adhikarana or philosophical topic is taken up for consideration by the author of the Brahma Sutras only to establish the validity and authoritative character of the Pancharatra doctrines. Sri Ramanuja's view looks quite logical and sound as sage Badarayana rejects all the Vaidic and Non-Vaidic schools of thought like Nyāya, Vaisesika, Sāṁkhya, Yoga, Purva Mimamsa, Bouddha, Jaina, and Pasupata as anti-Vedic. He takes up the consideration of the Pancharatra school as the last topic to prove the fact that its doctrines are authentic, authoritative and fully in accord with the Vedic revelations.

If Badarayana was not in agreement with the philosophical tenets of this school also, the question that will automatically arise is—Which philosophical school did the sage uphold in his Vedanta Sutras if he rejected all the prevalent systems? Evidently Badarayana seems to favour the Pancharatra school as its doctrines are fully in accord with the Vedas as the Agama tradition is of Vedic origin. George Thibaut the translator into English of *Sri Bhashya* says "The Sutrakāra closes the polemical section of the second chapter with a defense of the doctrine which inspite of objections, has to be viewed as the true one."

The Itihasas (epics), Sattvika Puranas (ancient accounts), Dharma-Shastras (code of ethics) and the Pancharatra Agamās (manual of worship) are as important as the Vedas themselves for knowing the intent and purport of the highest esoteric truths revealed in the Vedas. These supplementary scriptural texts are collectively called Smritis or what is remembered. It is common knowledge that the Smritis, which clarify the esoteric truths of the Vedas, are uncompromisingly monotheistic. The sage Badarayana himself refers to the Smritis frequently in his Brahma Sutras and so it should not be a matter of surprise if he is in favour of theistic interpretation of the philosophy of the Upanishads.

The various Vidyās or Upasanas on Brahman *i.e.* meditation and worship of Brahman are extensively dealt with in the Third Pada (Chapter) of the Brahma Sutras as the means for the realization of Brahman. Many consider the Upanishads are more concerned with Upasana or Worship and less with Yajña (Karma) or Jñāna (scriptural knowledge). Intellectual attraction and spiritual repulsion cannot be conducive to spiritual progress. The Vidyās or Upasanas have in view the One and only Supreme Being Vishnu of the Vedas and the Katha Upanishad as the sole object of meditation and worship. The Purusha Sukhta specifically declares that only by knowing the Purusha can one gain release or Moksha and there is no other way.

10) Essence of Pancharatra Doctrines

According to the Pancharatra school, Vasudeva the Supreme Lord is the material and efficient cause of the world. By worshipping Him exclusively (*i.e.* EKAYANA or worship of one Lord only), meditating on Him and knowing Him, the devotee of the Lord can attain liberation. Srimad Bhagawad Gita also teaches the Pancharatra doctrine of exclusive worship of Vasudeva the Supreme Lord. The origin of the Pancharatra system, which seems to be very ancient is shrouded in deep mystery. Some say that EKHAYANA (*i.e.* loyalty to Supreme Lord) is a sect of the KANVA Sakha of the Shukla (white) Yajur Veda. In fact, the word EKHAYANA seems to have been derived from the passage *NANYA PANTHA AYANAYA VIDYATE* *i.e.* "there is no other path", which occurs in the Purusha Sukhta of the Rig-Veda. There is a specific mention of EKHAYANA Sakha in the Seventh Chapter of the Chandogya Upanishad.

Some erudite philosophers hold the view that the Pancharatra doctrines could be associated with the Purusha Sukhta of the Rig-Veda and the Sathapatha Brahmana of the Shukla Yajur Veda. The earliest occurrence of the term PANCHARATRA is traced by researchers to a passage in the Satapatha Brahmana where Purusha Nārayana is reported to have conceived the idea of a PANCHARATRA SATTA, which is believed to be performance of sacrifices for five days as a means of obtaining superiority over all beings and becoming all beings. In fact, a preceding passage in the same Brahmana narrates in detail how Purusha Narayana by sacrificing Himself became the whole world. It is interesting to note that the same idea is conveyed in the Purusha Sukhta, which declares PURUSHA EVEDAGUM SARVAM: "Purusha has become everything". It is quite evident from these passages that Narayana of the Yajur Veda is the Purusha of the Purusha Sukhta in the Rig-Veda. So the opinion of scholars that the Pancharatra doctrines are wholly of Vedic origin only are well founded and very sound based on scriptural testimony. Incidentally, Ahirbudhnya Samhita a Pancharatra Agama explains the five stanzas of the Purusha Sukhta using the Vyuha or manifested form of Vasudeva indicating thereby that Vasudeva of the Pancharatra is none other than the Purusha of the Rig-Veda.

The extant Pancharatra literature spread over several Samhitas is believed to be based almost exclusively on the Gita, the Narayaniya section in the Santi Parva of the epic Mahabharata and the contents of Vaishnava Puranas. The period assigned to the extant Samhitas is not earlier than 5th century A.D. Srimad Bhagawad Gita which is patently based on the Pancharatra doctrines and accepted as one of the three basic scriptures of Vedanta can possibly be considered as the earliest available literature of the Pancharatra school apart from the Narayaniya section in the Mahabharata. The psalms of the Vaishnava saints of South India called Alvars which escaped destruction thanks to the action taken by Sriman Nathamunigal the earliest Sri Vaishnava Acharya for their careful preservation fills to some extent the vital gaps in knowledge about the theistic Vedanta. Some Vaishnava Upanishads and Puranas based on the Pancharatra system is also of considerable help in filling the gaps in the knowledge of theistic Vedanta. However, despite the gaps in knowledge the unalterable fact remains that Vaishnavism or the exclusive worship of Lord Vishnu as the only Supreme Being without a second must have had its origin in the Rig Vedic time based probably on the Purusha Sukhta hymn.

Incidentally, it is interesting to note that a fine blend of the Nigama and Agama traditions is found in the Vedic daily ritual of Sandhyavandhana performed thrice every day by all those who wear the sacred thread called the Yajnopavitha. The ritual begins with the sipping of water and touching the various parts of the body by uttering the fifteen divine names of Lord Vishnu and the ritual ends with dedication of all actions of the mind,speech and body to Supreme Lord Narayana with the words KAYENA VACHA MANASENDRIYAIVA. The Vedic seers who laid down this daily ritual must have had implicit faith in the Agama tradition that even the very utterance of the divine names of the Supreme Lord Vishnu thrice every day can have the sanctifying effect of removing all sins.

11) **Five Forms of Manifestation of Lord**

The Pancharatra School believes that the Supreme Lord manifests Himself in five different forms for the benefit of His devotees. These forms are 1) Para, 2) Vyuha, 3) Vibhava, 4) Antaryamin and 5) Archa. Each one of these five forms is briefly described below:

a) Para Roopa

Para is the transcendental form of the Supreme Lord in His Highest Abode called the Parama Pada, which the Vedas refer to as VISHNOR YAD PARAMAM PADAM. The manifested Para form of the Supreme Lord is meant only for the rendering of devotional service by those who are residents in the Paramapada called the Nitya Suris or the eternally free celestials and the Mukhtas or those souls released from bondage. This form is, therefore, not open to the mortal people of the mundane world.

b) Vyuha Roopa

From the Puranas it is learnt that the Devas or demigods when in serious trouble approach Brahma the First-born and seek ways to mitigate their woes. The gods headed by Brahma reach the Milky Ocean where the Supreme Lord Vishnu is resting in His serpent couch in Yoga Nidra or meditative sleep. The main purpose of manifestation in the Vyuha form seems to be to provide an opportunity to the Vedic gods to experience the blissful presence of the Lord so as to render devotional service to Him and also to get a redressal of their grievances. Neither the Upanishads nor Srimad Bhagawad Gita make any explicit mention of the Vyuha manifestation. However, Sri Vishnu Sahasranama in the Mahabharatha refers to the four different forms of Vyuha manifestations under the names of Vasudeva, Samkarshana, Pradyumna and Aniruddha. Each Vyuha form is believed to be connected with certain specific functions such as creation, sustenance, and dissolution of the world and the promulgation of spiritual knowledge. This form is not available for ordinary humans who have to be satisfied with the Para and the Vyuha forms portrayed in images and murtis.

c) Vibhava Avatara

The descent of the Supreme Lord by way of incarnations is called Avatara. The need and purpose of such incarnations in various forms are detailed in a nutshell in verses 7 and 8 of Chapter IV of the Gita where the Lord says "Arjuna, whenever there is a decline of righteousness and unrighteousness takes the upper hand I embody Myself in incarnations; for the protection of the virtuous and the destruction of the wicked as also to re-establish Dharma I take birth from age to age. The concept of Avatara or incarnations seems to have its origin in the Purusha Sukhta of the Rig-Veda in the passage AJAYAMANO BAHUDA VIJAYATE: "the birthless One manifests Himself in several incarnations."

The two Itihasas (epics) namely Ramayana and the Mahabharata as also the Sattvika Puranas describe in great detail the exploits of the Supreme Lord in His various incarnations. Neither Brahma the first-born nor the various Vedic gods can take Avatara and this seems to be the exclusive privilege of the Supreme Lord.Vishnu only who has under His exclusive control both Prakriti (matter) and Purusha (conscious souls). This fact itself is adequate proof of the supremacy of Lord Vishnu over all the other Vedic gods. The number of Avataras varies in various Puranas but the Dasavathara or the ten main incarnations of the Lord are the most popular and widely accepted. In the Sri Venkatesha Sahasranama Archana performed everyday to the Lord of the Seven Hills, His exploits in these Avataras find a prominent place among the thousand names of the Lord.

The doctrine of Avataras or descent of the Supreme Lord in various incarnations is basically a concept of the Agama tradition originating in the Purusha Sukhta in the Rig-Veda. The Satapatha Brahmana of the Shukla Yajur Veda refers to incarnations of the Supreme Lord in the fish, tortoise, boar and dwarf forms. The Katha Upanishad also seems to make an oblique reference to Vamana the dwarf form. The concept of Avatara found in the Agama tradition is, therefore, wholly of Vedic origin. Vibhava or descents of the Lord has its particular time and place and this form is available only to those who are contemporaries during the period of these Avataras. Others have to console themselves by hearing or reading about the exploits of the Lord from the epics and Puranas.

d) Antaryamin Form

The term Antaryamin refers to the indwelling spirit form of the Supreme Lord who is immanent in all His creations. Almost all the Upanishads refer to the indwelling Spirit form of the All-pervasive Lord as Bhutatma or Sarvantaratma etc. This also shows that the Antaratma concept is of Vedic origin. In fact, in the Antayami Brahmana of the Brihad Aranyaka Upanishad, it is declared that Brahman

(Creator) as the inner Self controls everything from within but neither the sentient nor the non-sentient entities are able to know the divinity, which lies concealed within.them. The Katha and the Mundaka Upanishads declare that the Lord of the size of thumb resides in a very subtle form in the inner recess of the human heart for the purpose of meditation in order to realize Him by His grace.

As the Antaryamin, the Supreme Lord residing in the heart assumes a subtle divine personal form to enable the devotee to meditate on Him. In verse 47 of chapter VI of the Gita the Lord declares that amongst all the Yogis he who devoutly worships Him with mind wholly fixed on Him is considered the best.

e) Archa Avatara

The words ARCHA AVATARA denote the descent of the Supreme Lord in image or murti form for adoration, prayer, propitiation and worship. Of all the forms of the Lord, the Archa or murti form is considered to be of supreme importance for the masses as it is visible and easily accessible for worship and surrender by one and all irrespective of caste, creed or level of purity. Formless or attributeless Brahman (Creator), besides being incomprehensible, reduces the spiritual practice into a sterile, soulless and tedious exercise. Name and form are indispensable for the human mind to grasp the Ultimate Reality of the Vedas. Murtis and images are the most favourable means for the concentration of mind for worship and meditation. Image worship serves the very useful purpose of prompting religious fervor, stimulating devotion and creating a spiritually elevating divine atmosphere.

Religion is essentially based on emotion and inspired by faith. The glorious, beautiful, smiling and enchanting form of the charming Lord evokes admiration, reverence and love as the automatic and immediate response of the human heart at the very sight of the murti. Basic human nature is the feeling of love towards some object or some person and so bhakti or loving devotion is very close to the human heart. Love, adoration, praise, prayer propitiation, worship and surrender are the various ways of expression of divine love and murtis serve as the best means for the practice of Bhakti. Very few can raise to the high level of mental worship and so the external worship of the Lord in visible and accessible form of murtis or images is considered the best for the common people. The Archa form is not remote and inaccessible like the Para or Vyuha forms or relates to the distant past like the Vibhava but is available here and now for worship and adoration in the immediate present. The Supreme Lord moved by the devout and ardent entreaties of His devotees, manifests Himself in consecrated murti forms in the DIVYA DESHAS or sanctified places for the purpose of worship and propitiation by His devotees. The lovely personality of the Supreme Lord with adornments and all auspicious attributes like beauty, effulgence, valour, etc. is personally experienced by the devout in the sacred image. The Moola Vigraha or main deity in the Sanctum Sanctorum of the temple is fixed and immobile made generally of stone or salagrama. The Utsava Murti or the festival deity used for being taken out of the Sanctum Sanctorum during festival times is generally made of alloys of metals like Gold, silver, copper, brass etc called Pancha loka. In the temple at Puri the image of Lord Jagannath is made of wood and is replaced every twelve years. The Main deity or Moolavar may be in the sitting or standing Para form or in the reclining Vyuha form but the festival deity Utsavar is generally in the standing posture only. The Para, and the Vyuha forms of manifestation of the Supreme Lord are beyond the reach of common people while the Vibhava or incarnated Avatara form can be personally witnessed only by those lucky few who are alive at the time and place of the Avatara or descent in incarnated form. The Antaryamin or the indwelling spirit form of the Lord cannot be perceived by the outward bound senses and is reserved only for the yogis who can turn their mind inwards to feel the divine presence of the Lord within them. Merciful, omnipresent and all pervasive Supreme Lord makes His divine presence felt by being manifest in a finite form in the Archa Vigraha or murti form to favour His sincere devotees. The Infinite Lord assumes a divine form to be present in the murti to enable His devotees to love, pray, worship and prostrate before Him to be relieved of their burdens. The worship of murtis purifies the mind and elevates the soul to a higher plane of consciousness and existence. The Archa form has, therefore, tremendous religious significance.

12) **Origin of Image Worship**

To many it may come as a surprise that the Vedic religion was not confined only to propitiation of gods through oblations in consecrated fire but allowed the worship of the Supreme Being in His personal form in images. The worship of images seems to date back to very ancient period and so tracing its origin may be difficult, if not, impossible. Some scholars believe that the passage in the Purusha Sukhta, TASYATWASHTA VIDADAT ROOPAMETI, i.e., "the divine architect gave form to the formless icon". They feel that this passage may possibly refer to the image worship in the Vedic times. In their considered view, some other passages in the Srutis (Vedas) seem to refer to image worship. For example, the passage HRIDA MANISHA MANASA ABHIKLITAHA: "to please the devotees, the Supreme Lord assumes form." The declaration YUKTAGRAVA JAYATE DEVA KAMAHA: "the playful Lord assumes the form of icon to bless His devotees", may relate to murti worship in the Vedic times.

The belief that image worship was unknown in the Vedic times is also disproved by the findings of images of gods and goddesses among the several seals dug out during the excavation at the Mohenjodaro and Harappa sites. The findings from the Indus Valley civilization provide adequate testimony to the irrefutable fact that the people in the Vedic period did worship images of deities. It is quite possible that the common people in the Vedic period must have found the fire sacrifices too cumbersome, complicated, time-consuming, ritualistic and expensive. Furthermore, such Yajnas (sacrifices) needed auspicious time and clean place for their performance besides physical and mental purity of all concerned with the performance. In fact, indifferent or careless performance and even incorrect pronunciation of the Vedic hymns was fraught with the risk of contrary results. Besides, the results yielded by the performance of such sacrifices were found to be temporary and evanescent and had to be periodically repeated.

Offering of worship to visible and easily accessible images of Brahman must have been found far easier of practice and did not cause any harm to any living beings or yield contrary results. The heart of devout souls must have found peace and happiness in the immediate present through the worship of images. These thoughts are not idle speculations but concrete facts based on scriptural testimony. In verse 7 of Section ii of Chapter II, the Mundaka Upanishad seems to voice its dissatisfaction in regard to Vedic sacrifices with the word "Verily, these sacrifices with their eighteen members (16 priests, the performer of sacrifice and his wife)are frail rafts on which such inferior work devoid of knowledge rests. The unwise who acclaim these sacrifices as the highest good certainly fall again and again into the domain of old age and death." The Upanishad unambiguously decries the fire sacrifices and its utter futility in the attainment of liberation. Lord Sri Krishna also in verses 42 to 44 of Chapter II of the Gita refers to the unwise who rejoice in the letter of the Vedic sacrifices thinking that there is nothing higher.

The Supreme Lord further refers to His worship in His personal form in images with fruit or flower and prostration in the following verses of Srimad Bhagawad Gita:

Chapter IV-verse 1—"Howsoever men approach Me, in

the same manner do I favour them; men verily follow My path in all ways."

Chapter VII—verse 21—"If any devotee seeks to worship with faith in any form, I make that faith steadfast in that form alone."

Chapter IX-verse 26—"Whosoever offers Me in true devotion a leaf, a flower, a fruit or even water, I accept the offering of that devotee who is pure of heart."

Chapter IX-verse 34—"Fix your mind on Me, be My devotee, worship Me and prostrate to Me; having thus controlled yourself and regarding Me as your supreme goal, you shall come to Me."

The words of Mundaka Upanishad and Bhagvad Gita very clearly indicate that people in the Vedic and epic period must have gradually lost faith in the efficacy of Yajnas or Vedic sacrifices and must have opted in favour of worship of the murti which must have gained wide currency in the Vedic period itself.

Moksha is not the exclusive prerogative or privilege of the upper castes only. Accusation of non-Vedic character of the Agama tradition during the Purana period in particular could have possibly emanated from the higher castes as the Pancharatra school advocated salvation to all those, irrespective of caste or creed, who exclusively devoted themselves to the worship of Vasudeva the Supreme Lord. In fact, the Vedas themselves prescribed the four Purusharthas or goals of life namely Dharma (righteousness), Artha (acquisition of wealth), Kama(fulfillment of desires) and Moksha(salvation) as the common goals of all the four castes. The Pancharatra doctrine of liberation irrespective of caste, sex or creed, through exclusive worship of Supreme Lord Vasudeva has in fact been reiterated by Lord Sri Krishna in verse 32 of chapter IX of Srimad Bhagavad Gita which is one of the three canonical scriptures of Vedanta.

Among the twelve Alvars, the Sri Vaishnava saints of South India, one was a woman and only two belonged to the upper varna. Nammalwar who is the most respected among all the Alvars and Tondaradipodiazhwar, a Brahmin by birth, in one of their psalms say that caste or creed has no place in the worship of the Supreme Lord for the attainment of salvation. The Law of Karma can be made inoperative by the Lord as His Grace can override the operation of all laws. Self-efforts at changing one's destiny can be of no avail as salvation is impossible of attainment without the willing consent of the Lord of Immortality. Pancharatra doctrine on salvation is based on the sanguine principle that the Grace of the Lord is far more potent and powerful than the non-sentient Law of Karma. Both the Katha and the Mundaka Upanishads emphasize the importance of Grace so essential for the attainment of Brahman. Purusha Sukta of the Rig-Veda declares that there is no other way to salvation than the knowledge of Purusha.

13) Significance of Murti Worship

Skeptics, who have no faith in the worship of sacred images, are very highly critical of this practice without a proper understanding of the rationale, value and benefit that can accrue out of such practice. The criticism that murti worship is primitive, excessively anthropomorphic reducing Godhead to the human level etc., are based on several misconceptions about murti worship. God is certainly not the image but He sanctifies the image by being present in it. The image is not a mere symbol but the very person of God who makes Himself available for worship to His devotees through His presence in the image. The image is not the representation of a soulless anthropomorphic being, but the very Cosmic Lord Himself. The adornments and the insignia are the different aspects of His creative process. For example, the discus is the mind, the conch the ego, the jewel Kaustubha the individual soul, Nandaka the sword is the knowledge and its sheath is the ignorance that envelops the knowledge.

The mental feeling with which the worship of the murti is done is far more important than the physical object of worship. The object of worship is the Supreme Lord and not the image. Ardent devotees actually feel the divine presence of the Lord in the visible and the easily accessible image and are relieved of their heart's burden. Ignorant people who do not understand the deep spiritual significance of murti worship can never appreciate the immense benefits that can flow out of such worship. Those who see only the stone in the sacred image can never see the presence of the Lord while those who feel the divine presence of the Lord do not see the stone at all. How the murti is viewed by the human mind is the most important aspect of murti worship.

The mental block of the skeptics veil the divine presence in the sacred image depriving them of the divine feeling which the devotees experience. Devotees who feel the presence of the Supreme Lord in the murti weep, shout in joy, pour out their heart in love and surrender themselves heart and soul to the murti, deriving peace and happiness in the process. Reverence, humility, sincerity, devotion etc., to the very person of the Lord experienced in the image helps the cleansing of the mind, the purification of the soul and the elevation of consciousness to a higher state of existence. The predominant thought in the mind of the devotee is of prayer and worship as the real object of his worship is the Supreme Lord and not the physical murti. The image is viewed by the devotees as the manifestation of the Lord Himself and not as His symbol or representation. The mental state overshadows the object worshipped. The devotee knows that the Infinite All-pervasive Lord is present in the murti for the purposes of worship but He is not the murti itself. Only those devotees in the proper mental state of worship can derive the full benefit of murti worship.

The high mental state of the devotees can be personally witnessed in Tirumala. Thousands of devotees wait patiently in long queue for hours just to catch a momentary glance of the bewitching and ever smiling Supreme Lord who is always willing to lend His ears to hear the grievances of His devotees and extend His protection to them. The fatigue and tediousness of the journey and the long hours of wait are totally forgotten on entering the Garbha Graha or the Sanctum Sanctorum. During the few seconds they are in front of the deity they experience the spiritual vibrations that emanate from the divine presence of the Lord. The shouts of 'GOVINDA, GOVINDA reverberate in the ears and everything else is forgotten. The very sight of the Lord elevates the soul to high plane of consciousness and they feel purer by being spiritually reinvigorated. By seeking the forgiveness of the Lord for their past sins they feel mentally purer and spiritually ennobled.

Devotees come from every nook and corner of the country travelling for days and they spend long hours in serpentine queue only to spend a few seconds in front of the Lord but they feel that this helps them in getting relieved of their physical and mental distress. For the practice of Ekantika Bhakti, or exclusive devotion to the Supreme Lord, the worship of sacred image is an indispensable necessity. People find immense peace and solace in murti worship than in Vedic fire sacrifices. The ignorant are the ones who do not know the value and efficacy of murti worship and who view this practice with suspicion. The formless and attributeless Brahman is very abstract, remote and incomprehensible for devout souls who feel attracted instantly to the easily accessible and visible sacred image, with name and form. People let out the divinity within them through music, dance, poetry, art, architecture etc and temples serve as ideal medium for this purpose. The annual BRAHMOTSAVAM festival is an occasion for the devotees to show their deep love for the Lord by serving Him with whatever talents they possess. Love is the natural emotion of human beings and murti worship ideally facilitates the cultivation of love to their personal Lord with form for the practice of Bhakti.

As stated earlier, image worship has been in vogue from very ancient time and is wholly of Vedic origin. One of the hymns of Rig-Veda makes an explicit mention of the worship of the murti of the Supreme Lord to get relieved of the past sins. It will not, therefore, be right to say that the Vedas are against the worship of images. The Pancharatra concept of Archavatara forms the very foundation for the worship of images. Of the consecrated images, the SWAYAM VYAKTA or the self-manifested sacred images are considered the most important and sacred. The murtis in the temples at Srirangam and Tirumala are believed to be the manifestation of the Supreme Lord out of His own volition and will in the form of icon.(SWAYAM VYAKTA).

14) **Antiquity of Tiruengadam**

Out of the 108 Divya Deshams or places sanctified by Divine presence, Srirangam and Tirumala occupy the pride of place as the murtis there are believed to be SWAYAM VYAKTA or self-manifested. The glory and greatness of the Supreme Lord residing in the Seven Hills have been described in the Deva Bhasha Sanskrit in the Srutis and the Smritis. Sanskrit is called Deva Bhasha or divine language as the Lord's divine revelations have been in Sanskrit. Some believe that the spoken language of the Devas or demi-gods is Sanskrit and so that language is called Deva Bhasha.

Tracing the origin of the Archa or image form at Tirumala is beyond the realm of human possibility as the image is SWAYAM VYAKTA or self-manifested out of Lord's own volition. No one, therefore, knows the origin of Tiruvengadam. It may have been in existence right from the Vedic times and must have gained wide popularity during the period of the Puaranas. Some believe that the image at Tirumala must be as ancient as the Rig Veda as, in their opinion, the passage (X-153-1) asks the sinful to visit Venkatachala to get rid of their sins through the words VIKATE GIRIM GACHHA.

In the Venkatachala Purana the same words find a place. Another verse found in the Paramarthika Upanishad says KAKUTRE VIKATAYA PITRE SWAHA, which means " I surrender my soul to the Lord of Venkatachala."

Twelve Puranas including the Brahmanda, Bhavishyottara, Skanda, Garuda, Padma, Markhandeya, Vamana and Varaha have glorified at length the greatness of the Supreme Lord at Tirumala. In fact, the Varaha Purana goes to the extent of saying that in the entire world there is no Divya Desha like Tiruvengadam and there is no God equal to the Lord in the serpent couch and further adds that there is no God or wealth or Kula Devatha (family Deity) or Parama Gathi (Highest goal) equal to Venkatachala. In the same Purana the term VENKATA is defined as SARVAPAPANI VEM PRAHUHU KATA i.e. "the place which burns up all sins." In the Vamana Purana, the passage AMRITA AISWARYA SAMATWAT VENKATADRI ITISMRITAHA, *i.e.*, "Venkatadri is remembered as the place conferring wealth and immortality." Nammalwar, the most respected Sri Vaishnavite Alvar, in a psalm beginning with the words VEMKADANGAL, says that all the debts owed are cleared. In other words the Lord redeems all the sins and grants security and wellbeing. T.T.D. Authorities have done a great service to the devotees of Lord Venkatesa by bringing together all the relevant passages from the various scriptures and presenting them in the form of a book entitled SRI VENKATACHALA MAHATHMYAM.

15) Eternal message Conveyed by Lord Srinivasa

A close look at the Moola Vigraha or Main Deity and the Utsava Murthy or Festival Deity at Tirumala will reveal that His right hand is directed downwards to His Lotus Feet while His left hand in the Katya Valambita posture with the palm resting on the left thigh below the hip indicating His protection for those who seek His refuge. For the Sri Vaishnavas, Prapatti or Saranagathi *i.e.* surrender is considered the most efficacious means for gaining the Grace of the

Supreme Lord. In verse 66 of Chapter XVIII of Srimad Bhagavad Gita, Lord Sri Krishna declares "Abandoning all duties, come to Me alone for refuge; I will relieve you from all sins; grieve not." This verse is called by the Sri Vaishnavites as the CHARAMA SLOKA or the final message of the Lord. In the Purusha Sukhta, the Parama Purusha is called UTAMRITATSYESANAHA *i.e.* the Lord of Immortality as only He can confer Immortality and none of the other Vedic gods. The very word Venkata means freedom from all sins by seeking forgiveness of the Lord through surrender. The eternal message conveyed by the Archa form at Tirumala, is the teaching imparted by Lord Sri Krishna in the CHARAMA SLOKA of Srimad Bhagavad Gita.

The biography of Sri Ramanuja reveals that during his halcyon days, people of rival faiths out of spite and jealousy at the popularity of Sri Vaishnavism claimed that the murti at Tirumala was not of the Supreme Lord Vishnu. Sri Ramanuja is reported to have countered these false claims by citing passages from Rig-Veda, Sattvika Puranas, etc. to prove beyond any shadow of doubt that the image of the Lord residing in the Seven Hills is of Lord Vishnu only. The eternal message conveyed by gesticulation in the Moolava and the Utsava archanas of the Lord seems to give lie to the claims of those who say that the image is not of the Supreme Lord. Besides, the psalms of Alvars and several passages in the Puranas prominently bring out the fact that the image at Tirumala is of Tirumal the Supreme Lord Vishnu only. Several songs of the Haridasas of Karnataka and those of Annamacharya of Andhra also highlight this fact.

16) **Alvars and Lord Venkatesa**

The Sri Vaishnava Saints of South India are called Alvars. The term AZHWARS OR ALVARS refer to those saintly souls who were steeply immersed in the exclusive devotion and worship of Lord Vishnu. Through their Tamil psalms on the various deities in the Divya Deshas or consecrated places they proclaimed the supremacy of Lord Vishnu. They prominently brought out the greatness of His divine deeds as also His beauty, valour, perfections, mercy, grace, etc., through their songs in the vernacular. As the pioneers of theistic Vedanta they were thoroughly familiar with the inner purport of the Vedas, Upanishads, Itihasas, Puranas, as also the Pancharatra doctrines. They popularized the message of Vedic Vaishnavism through their ecstatic devotional outpourings in the language of the masses which even to this day are memorized by their followers and recited in Vaishnava temples. The psalms of the Azhwars are regarded as equivalent to the Vedic hymns and used in Vaishnavite temples along with the Vedas.

To the Alvars the Supreme Lord was not a sectarian deity of Vaishanavism but the Universal Lord revealed in the Vedas. These saints, as the supreme devotees of Lord Vishnu, were the foremost amongst the Sri Vaishnava Acharyas (teachers). They propagated Sri Vaishnavism by bringing out the message of theistic Vedanta to the notice of the masses through their poetical works highlighting the divine glory and deeds of Lord Vishnu in His various Avataras. As Dravida Veda *i.e.* Tamil Veda their psalms bring out the essence of the Srutis (Vedas) and Smritis (supplementary texts) for the benefit of the common folks. Sri Vaishnavism follows Ubhaya Vedanta or two Vedanta philosophies namely the Tamil and the Sanskrit Vedas. The chanting of the Lord's Divine Names, meditation of His Archa (sacred image) and Avatara (incarnated) forms and worship in the Divya Deshas or sanctified places have been the basic message of the Alvars in their psalms which are collectively called the Nalayira Divya Prabhandam or the 4,000 divine songs.

Ten Alvars have together sung 195 songs in praise of the Supreme Lord of the Seven Hills. The largest number of compositions, 63 in all, have been composed by Tirumangai

Alvar while only two verses have been rendered by Tiruppan Alvar who makes a passing reference to Tirumala in his poetical work in praise of the Lord in Srirangam. The first three Alvars collectively known as the Mudal Alvars who have composed a hundred songs each on the glory and greatness of Sriman Narayana have sung several songs in praise of Lord Venkatesa. Poigai Alvar the first among the three has sung 10, Bhutatazhwar the second has sung 9 while the third called Peyazwar has rendered as many as 19 verses in praise of the deity of Tirumala. All the Alvars describe the natural beauty of Tiruvengadam, the importance of the place and the glory of the Supreme Lord there.

Nammalvar who is the most prominent of all the Alvars in one of his 44 psalms in praise of Lord Venkatesa, says that the entire life time should be spent in ceaseless loving service of the Supreme Lord at Tirumala. Peyalvar refers to Venkadathan as VEDATTHAN meaning thereby that the Lord of the Seven Hills is the One Supreme Lord and the Ultimate Truth of the Vedas. Poigai Alvar calls Venkadam as MAL UGANDA VUR *i.e.* "the Abode most liked by the Supreme Lord." Bhudatazhwar refers to Lord Venkatesa as VEDATHAN VENKADATHAN VINNOR MUDI THOYUM PADATHAN, which means that the prostrating Devas or gods worship the Lotus Feet of the Parama Purusha of the Vedas residing in Tirumala with bowed head. In the eleven very poignant and most moving verses rendered by Kulasekhara Alvar, who is believed to be the author of the most popular devotional hymn called Mukunda Mala, the saint prays to the Lord that he should be either an insect or a bird or a fish or vessel or flower or tree or river or region or path or step or at least some object in the hill of Tirumala. The psalms of the Alvars on Lord Venkatesa are full of piety and bring out in lyrically beautiful Tamil the greatness and glory of the hills and the Lord which cannot be recaptured in translation.

Incidentally, it is interesting to note that even though

Tondaradipodi Alvar has not rendered any song on Lord Venkatesa, his Tirppalliezhutchi, which is a garland of 11 verses to wake up the Lord of Srirangam, is recited before Lord Venkatesa in the Dhanur Masa, *i.e.*December-January, in place of the regular Sri Venkatesa Suprabhatham. This only goes to show that the Lord at Srirangam and at Tirumala are the self same Supreme Lord of the Vedas.

17) **Acharyas and Lord Srinivasa**

In verse 5 of Canto 90 of the devotional poem called *Narayaneeyam*, the author Meppattur Narayana Bhattadri says "The great Sankaracharya who is termed Bhagavan to indicate his divinity, has done special honour to Thee (Narayana) among all the deities, though in his philosophy he had no particular loyalty to any deity. He has interpreted the Sri Vishnu Sahasranama and other works as devoted exclusively to Thee and in the end he passed away uttering Thy praise." In the introduction to the musical rendering of the famous Bhaja Govindam song by Smt. M.S.Subbalakshmi, Rajaji in his brief talk in English says that Sri Adi Sankara who drank the ocean of knowledge (*Jñāna*) rendered in his later years devotional hymns to show that *Bhakti* (devotion) and *Jñāna* (knowledge) are one and the same. It is a well known fact that the great Acharya composed several hymns in praise of Lord Vishnu like the Shatpathi stotram, Bhaja Govindam etc., besides devotional songs in praise of Lord Krishna, Hari, Mukunda, Panduranga etc.

Of all the devotional hymns of Sri Adi Sankara, the Bhaja Govindam is possibly the most popular. According to Rajaji. the Acharya has packed into the Bhaja Govindam song the essence of Vedanta. In the Hymn, the Acharya asks us to worship Govinda as, at the hour of death, the rules of grammar can be of no avail. The mind of the great Acharya is more clearly revealed in one of the stanzas of Carpata-Panjarika stotram where it is said " Recite Gita, chant the thousand names of Lord Vishnu, meditate on

SREEPATHI ROOPAM. It is common knowledge that Lord Govinda is the SREEPATHI extolled in the Sri Vishnu Sahasranama and propitiated in image form in Tirumala as Sreenivasa.

Four

BENGAL VAISNAVISM

Opposition to the nondualism of Šaṅkara—Agreement with the earlier schools of Vaiṣṇvism—Distinction form other schools of Vaiṣṇavism—Concept of Brahman—Emphasis on the concept of sweetness of Brahman—Attributes and power of Brahman recognised—Māyā as a real power—Relation between Brahman sand Māyā—Relation between Brahman and the world—The new category of *Acintya bhedābheda*—The position of *Avikṛtapriṇāmavādā*—The finite souls as manifestations of *Jivaśakti*—The world as both a snare and a house of correction for the deluded finite spirits—Destiny of the Jīva—Dawn of *Bhakti*—The highest type of Bhakti—Ultimate reality revealed in the *Hlādinī* aspect of the *Svarūpaśakti*—Rādhā and Kṛṣṇa identified with the Hlādinī and the ultimate reality respectively—Hyphenated nature of Rādhā and Kṛṣṇa—Kṛṣṇa identified with *Rasa*—The four varieties of ideal love in *Vraja*—The *Kāntābhāva*—Its progress towards *Mahābhāva*—Gopīs and Rādhā—Rādhā's love for Kṛṣṇa—Rādhā and Kṛṣṇa as two inseparable aspects of the integral reality—The highest reality distinguished from Brahman and Paramātman—Love as the means of attaining the highest reality—Essential nature of the ultimate reality in *Rāsalīlā* (amorous sport in the highest level of transcendental plane).

Like four other earlier schools of Vaiṣṇavism, the Bengal school founded by the followers of Caitanaya vehemently opposes Śaṅkara's interpretation of Brahman as one differenceless powerless, attributeless, inactive and impersonal reality and Māyā as the inexplicable cause of the illusory appearance of the world of plurality on the substratum of Brahman. No less strong is its onslaught on the Śaṅkarite doctrine of absolute identity of Jīva with Brahman, the finite with the Infinite, the imperfect with the perfect, which appears simply preposterous to the Vaiṣṇavas of all sects. But while joining hands with other schools of Vaiṣṇavism in combating Śaṅkara's interpretation of Brahman, Māyā, Jīva and their relation, this school has developed some important features that distinguish it not merely from the Advaitism (non-dualism) of Śaṅkara but also from the theistic systems of the earlier Vaiṣṇavas.

Relying chiefly on the authority of the Vedas, all the schools of Vedāntism regard Perception, Inference and other sources of valid knowledge as useful only in so far as they expound the nature of the ultimate reality consistently with the teachings of the Vedas, and the Bengal school is not exception to them in this respect. One special feature of the Bengal school, however, is its inclusion of the *Srīmad-bhāgavata-purāṇa* within the scope of revealed scriptures and acceptance of the same as the genuine commentary on the *Brahma-sūtra*. The mode of interpretation of the scriptural texts adopted by this school widely differs from that Śaṅkara who, to suit his purpose, has chiefly resorted to the secondary meaning of the scriptural texts even when their primary meaning is quite admissible. It is on the primary meaning of the texts that the Bengal school has laid its emphasis, the secondary meaning being allowed only in cases of failure of all unbiased attempts at interpretation by reference to the primary meaning. The mode interpreting the scriptural texts by reference to the secondary meaning, it has been pointed out, is hardly consistent with the Vedāntic theory of intrinsic validity of the revealed scriptures. Since all secondary meanings are by nature inferential, to resort to them is to rely on inference and reject the self-authoritativeness of the scriptures.

Following the teachings of the Upaniṣads, the Bengal

School regards Brahman who is 'one without a second' as the ultimate reality, the real source and ground of the universe. An insight into the etymological meanings of the word Brahman reveals that Brahman Himself is great and He can make others great. He is not attributeless, powerless, inactive and impersonal as Śaṅkara supposes, but endowed with supramundane attributes, inconceivable powers, supernormal activities and divine personality. Since Brahman is infinite and all-perfect, no limit can be set to His power, attributes, activity and personality. There is none equal to Brahman, not to speak of any one being superior to Him. So far there is nothing essentially new in the conception of Brahman that distinguished it from the earlier schools of Vaiṣṇavism. What is remarkable about the conception of Brahman in this system is the distinction of His attributes into those expressive of majesty (*Aiśvaryya*) and those expressive of sweetness (*Mādhuryya*) with a view to laying emphasis on the latter. No doubt the attribute of sweetness has been ranked high also in the systems of Nimbārka and Vallabha who, unlike Rāmīnuja and Madhva, have conceived Brahman and His energy not as Nārāyana and Lakṣmī but as Kṛṣṇa and Rādhā in their eternal embrace of love, but in its analysis of the sweetness of the personality of Kṛṣṇa as increasingly revealed in His sports with young comrades, fond parents and dearest consorts, of whom Rādhā is the foremost, the Bengal school has gone far ahead of the schools of Nimbārka and Vallabha. Of the numerous powers of Brahman, *three*, *viz*., (1) the power relating to the creation of the world. (2) the power that manifests the Jīvas and (3) the power constituting His intrinsic nature, stand out prominent. On the authority of *Viṣṇupurāṇa* the power constituting the intrinsic nature is said to be the *Parā śakti* (the highest power), the power that manifests the Jīva (finite souls) is called *Kṣertrjñā* or *Jīva-śakti,* and the power that lies at the root of the world-process is designated *Avidyā-śakti* (*i.e.* nescience). The scriptural description of Brahman as *Saccidānanda* has been understood in this system not as the mere negation of nonbeing, absence of consciousness and absence of bliss as in the system of Śaṅkara, nor as the mere presence of the attributes of being, consciousness and bliss as in the system of theistic teachers is general, but as experience of the intrinsic power (*svarūpa-śakti*) of Brahman as distinguished from His other two powers. Brahman is essentially being, consciousness and bliss in as much as His true nature consists in eternally, exercising. His power in its three aspects known as *Sandhinī, Saṁvit* and *Hlādinī*. It is by the Sandhinī aspect of His Svarūpa-śakti (intrinsic power) that He upholds all existence including His own; the function of the Saṁvit aspect consists in enabling Him to know and make others know, while that of Hlādinī to enjoy delight and make others enjoy the same. Unlike Avidyā-śakti (otherwise known as Māyā-śakti) and Jīva-śakti (otherwise known as Taṭsthā-śakti), Savarūpa-śakti, being inherently spiritual, stands to Brahman in the closest relation of self-link (*Svarūpa-sam-vadha*). It is the locus of *Jīva-śakti* which manifests itself in the forms of innumerable limited spirits, and the *Jīva-śakti* in its turn is the locus of Māyā-śakti which finds its expression in the inanimate, insentient, material world. Being the manifestations of the *Svarūpa-śakti* in which they are rooted, *Jīva-śakti* and *Māyā-śakti* cannot be called unreal. They are ranked lower than *Svarūpa-śakti* in view of their incompetence to reveal Brahman fully. While Jīva-śakti reveals Him as the plurality of finite spirit and Māyā-śakti presents Him as the inanimate, insentient, material world of diversity, Saṁvit-sakti which is an aspect of His Svarūpa-śakti reveals Him as the all-inclusive spiritual unity. The highest and most perfect aspect of the Svarūpa-śakti which forms the ground of two other aspects as well as of all other saktis (powers) is *ananda* or bliss. This aspect of the Svarūpa-śakti is named Hlādinī which is by nature infinite and dynamic, and it is only as mirrored in His Hlādinī-śakti that Brahman is regarded as the ultimate reality in its most perfect form and termed Bhagavat whom the devotees seek to serve lovingly after the manner and under the care of some one of the four types of eternal associates who are included in the countless manifestations of His Svarūp-śakti in the transcendental plane.

Basing their arguments partly on spiritual experience and partly on logical principles, the advocates of the Bengal school have attempted to convince all people of the inadequacy and unsoundness of the conception of impersonal Brahman upheld by Śaṅkara and that of personal Brahman sponsored by the earlier Vaiṣṇavas. Śaṅkara is perfectly justified in thinking that the highest spiritual plane cannot be reached without transcending the various limitations of space and time, body and mind, desire and aversion, mine and thine, ego-consciousness and other consciousness to which the human soul is ordinarily subject and that so long as soul is dominated by ordinarily subject and that so long as the soul is dominated by ego-consciousness the conception of the ultimate reality formed by it must be partial and relative. But his conclusion that in order to attain the ultimate reality one must completely mere one's ego-consciousness or individuality in the same, does not commend itself to reason, for in case there is a total loss of individuality, there can be no direct experience of the nature of the ultimate reality. An experience of the true nature of the ultimate reality requires not merely the power of transcending the lower planes of experience from which the earlier Vaiṣṇavas have described the ultimate reality as the omnipotent, omniscient, infinite, enteral, perfectly good an perfectly benevolent person creating, sustaining, controlling, developing and destroying the world, but also a capacity for retaining the spiritual individuality in the highest plane of spiritual experience. If a spiritual aspirant fails to develop this capacity sufficiently through systematic self-discipline and culture of loving devotion, he cannot have access to the secret chambers of the highest spiritual edifice. Having transcended the plane of ordinary experience in the state of beautific trance (Samādhi), he loses his individuality in the overwhelming effulgence of one homogeneous, impersonal, differenceless consciousness and on his return to the plane of reason (Buddhi) regards this as the true character of the ultimate reality. The conception of the highest reality reached thus, though not altogether false, is only partial and as such falls far short of the idea formed on a closer and deeper acquaintance with it. The true nature of the supreme reality is agreedly above all phenomenal distinctions and limitation that belong to the domain of Māyā, but is not a homogeneous unity of supra-mundane consciousness devoid of all transcendental characteristics as Śaṅkara supposes, for the spiritual experience of the abler aspirants who after crossing the dazzling brilliance of the homogeneous unity of consciousness enter deeper through intense devotion, testify to the display of spiritual particulars (Viśeṣas) in the essential nature of the supreme reality. Viewed from the highest plane of spiritual experience, the supreme reality is possessed of a personality that both includes and transcends the absolutely differenceless, powerless and attributeless unity of consciousness commonly known as Brahman. Though infinite in the true sense of the term, the ultimate reality is not formless but possessed of spiritual figure (Vigraha) which manifests itself differently as *Brahman, Paramātman* and *Bhagavat* according to the capacities of the aspirants who seek to realise it. When an aspirant is blessed with the vision of the highest and most perfect manifestation of the figure which is identified with the Bhagavat, Brahman appears to him as a halo (*Atanubhā*), and Paramātaman as a part, both spiritual, thereof.

The unsoundness of the doctrine of one impersonal Brahman devoid of all powers and attributes appears all the more glaring when a logical explanation of the undeniable realities of the lower planes of experience is attempted. To call the realities of the lower planes of experience mere illusions in Brahman very much like those of snakes in ropes, suns in water, blueness in the sky etc., is to indulge in weak forms of analogy which cannot be relied on, for the points of difference between Brahman and the things of the world are far more numerous and important than those of resemblance between them. Brahman, the only reality, is devoid of all differences, external and internal, whereas each of the instances of illusion cited to draw the analogy implies more than one reality of the empirical order as also the possibility of extraneous reasons for the production of the illusion in question. The hypothesis of illusion can hardly be reconciled with that of the sole reality of differenceless impersonal Brahman, since illusion presupposes not only the presence of the substratum in which it appears but also the existence of those who fall in a prey to it. Besides, the direct experience of the manifold world with its wonderful order and adaptation, plan and purpose, beauty and grandeur prevents every rational mind from thinking that it is an illusion.

Since Brahman is the only reality according to the teachings of the Upaniṣads and since the reality of the world of finite minds and material objects is undeniable, Śaṅkara has to admit an inexplicable power of Brahman, viz., Māyā to account for the appearance of the different orders of the lower planes of experience. But according to him, Māyā, though appearing real to those who are within its range, has only a relative and phenomenal value to those who have reached the highest plane of spiritual experience where Brahman alone shines. For him, therefore, Brahman conceived in relation to Māyā has only a relative and phenomenal character which is not ultimately real. The Bengal school follows other schools of Vaiṣṇavism in combating this view of Śaṅkara and upholding the reality of Māyā and its products, while admitting that they are by nature subject to constant change. From the standpoint of worldly experience Brahman is best conceived as the eternal possessor of Māyā-śakti endlessly expressing Himself as the world of finite minds and material objects and enjoying the infinite glories and beauties of His infinite nature under self-imposed limitations. Indeed the earlier schools of Vaiṣṇavism have adhered to this conception of Brahman. But the Bengal school, instead of stopping with this as the highest conception of divine personality, proceeds further to have an acquaintance with the inner nature of that personality. According to this school, impersonal Brahaman of Śaṅkara is only an abstraction from the inner personality of Brahman, and the personal Brahman of the earlier schools of Vaiṣṇavism, an introduction to its outer nature.

Although the conception of Brahman as eternally and inherently possessed of a real power called Māyā is common to all the schools of Vaiṣṇavism, yet they are not unanimous in their views of the relation between Brahman and His Śakti (power). Śakti (power), however, is not directly known, but inferred from its expressions which are directly perceived. It is not self-existent, but dependent on its substratum. Māyā, being the Śakti of Brahman, is known through its expression in the form of the world of mind and matter and exists in, for and by Brahman who alone is its substratum. Since the *world* is inconceivable except as dependent on Māyā and the latter is incapable of being understood save as resting on Brahman, their identity cannot be denied. But this identity is not exclusive of difference, for while the manifestations of Māyā in the form of the world are many and perceptible. Māyā is essentially one and imperceptible, and while Māyā is transformed into the world, Brahman transcends it and remains unchanged in Himself. Thus there are two equally real aspects of the relation, *viz.*, *identity* and *difference,* neither of which should be given preference. Śaṇkara has emphasised the identity of Brahman, Māyā and the world to the extent of asserting that strictly speaking, Brahman, the differenceless, attributeless one, alone exists, and all else is illusion. Rāmānuja and Madhva have stressed the difference of the world from Māyā as also that of Māyā from Brahman and regarded Māyā and its products as real. Having no predilection for any one of the two aspects of identity and difference, the advocates of the Bengal school have conceived the relation of Brahman, Māyā and the world as one of *identity in difference and difference in identity* which has its strong support in the system of Nimbārka among the earlier systems of Vaiṣṇavism. Nimbārka and his followers think that Brahman, viewed as the undivided whole of Being, excluded the possibilities of any other independent reality and admits individual souls and matter only as dependent existences forming parts of the integrity. The relation between the *independently real* and the *dependently real,* between Brahman and the world of finite selves and matter, is one of non-difference in difference. Brahman is both different and non-different from the world of finite minds and material objects,—*different* because of His transcedent nature, independence and excellence in respect of expansiveness, wisdom and goodness, *non-different* because of His sustaining of it and immanence in it. The reduction of the dependent reals, *i.e.* finite selves and the material world, to śaktis (powers) of Brahman is, however, a noticeable feature of the Bengal school, for it marks an improvement upon the Nimbārka school in supporting the Vedāntic conception of the ultimate reality as one without a second. Fully conscious of the logical difficulty of reconciling the conception of identity of *śakti* (the power) and *śaktimān* (the possessor of power) with that of the difference between them, this school, instead of regarding one as real and the other as unreal, has had recourse to a category of relation which is supralogical and therefore inconceivable. The recognition of this category has been deemed indispensable for understanding the peculiar standpoint of this school named *Acintyabhedābheda* school which differs not only from the viewpoint of *Vivartavāda* upheld by Śaṅkara but also from that of *Parināmavāda* advocated by the earlier Vaiṣṇava schools. While according to *Vivartavāda* the world is an unreal appearance that cannot touch the real nature of Brahman, the Bengal school calls the world real as a house of spiritual training for the finite souls. Again, while in the *Pariṇāmavāda* of the Vaiṣṇavas the world and the finite souls are conceived as substantial modifications of Brahman Himself, the Bengal school regards them as the transformations of His *Śakti*. The standpoint of the Bengal school is called *Avikṛta-pariṇāmavāda,* since while saving the reality of the world of finite souls and material objects as real transformations of

Śakti which is real, this schools, because of its implicit fait in the unthinkable power of Brahman, finds no difficulty in leaving His integrity unimpaired. There is, however, no dearth of scriptural evidence in support of the unthinkable nature of Brahman. Since the *śakti* (power) of Brahman is different from Him, the transformation of the former into the finite souls and the material world does not affect the essence of the latter, and since *śakti* is non-different from Brahman, the finite souls and the material world are non-different from Brahman. The logical difficulty of conceiving Brahman as simultaneously different and non-different from His *Śakti* has led the advocates of this school to the view that they stand in the relation of unthinkable difference in non-difference. Since neither aspect of the relation can be ignored, and since it is incapable of being treated under either of the aspects, the relation between Brahman and His *Śakti* has been named the relation of *inconceivable difference-in-non-difference.*

While admitting its non-difference from Brahman, the Bengal school regards Māyā as His external power *(Bahiraṅgāśakti)* by which He conceals His essential nature and distorts Himself into the inanimate, insentient material world of many. The creation of the world and the beginningless delusion of the finite souls have been attributed to Māyā. The finite souls, being manifestations of the *jīva-śakti,* are at one different and non-different from Brahman. The non-difference of the *jīva-śakti.* from Brahman has been construed to mean that Brahman Himself has appeared in the form of finite selves and spirits through His *jīva-śakti.* Standing on the marginal line between Svarūpa-śakti and Māyā-śakti of Brahman, jīva-śakti (otherwise known as *Taṭsthā-śakti*) reveals of dual inclination for divine as well as mundane life. The finite souls have as much a right to citizenship in the world of Māyā as in the domain of Svarūpa-śakti. Because of their leaning towards Māyā they forget their real nature as dependent on and subservient to Brahman and regard themselves as independent personalities. One important function of Māyā in addition to that of causing the world-appearance is to ensnare the inclined souls by its allurements. But the finite soul cannot be doomed for ever, since on the one hand the world-appearance and the snare caused by Māyā, though real, are not permanent and on the other the finite souls sharing as they do the spiritual essence of Brahman never lose their power of extricating themselves from the clutches of Māyā. The miseries and failures repeatedly experienced in the world of Māyā serve to convince the finite souls of the worthlessness of the values attached to the objects of the material world and the demands of the ego, and awake them up to the divine way of life. On the dawn of spiritual enlightenment they begin to realise their real star as sparks thrown out by the internal reality and their true duty as subservience to it. This marks the beginning of *Bhakti,* a way of life quite consistent with the true nature of the finite self as self-dedicating and loving part of the spiritual whole. The acquaintance of the true nature, once formed through intellectual comprehension, gradually develops into an attitude of the entire being revealing itself in emotional and conative aspects of life. Intellectual recognition of the subservient nature of the soul and the spuriousness of its sense of self-assertion and independence, emotional urge for unconditional self-dedication and eternal love together with conative attempts at subordinating all finite will and finite values to the will of the *Infinite whole* enter into the life of *Bhakti.* This type of *Bhakti* which follows the true nature of the finite self is called *Rāgātmikā-bhakti* and is most highly appreciated by the Bengal school. The other type based on mere scriptural injunction in called *Vaidhī-bhakti* and ranked lower, since it is only a mechanical allegiance to the scriptures lacking in emotional fervour. The supreme reality can be fully known only by the highest form of Rāgātmikā-bhakti as represented in Rādhā's love for Kṛṣṇa.

The highest ideal of perfect love in which the ultimate reality is truly and fully reflected and without which the latter cannot be conceived, has been represented as the most preponderating aspect of its *svarūpa-śakti.* Rādhā has been identified with the *Hlādinī-śakti* (delighting power) of Kṛṣṇa, and the ultimate reality has been conceived not as Kṛṣṇa apart from Rādhā but as Kṛṣṇa and Rādhā eternally hyphenated, for the delighting power and the delighted, love and its objects, are by nature inseparable. The scriptural description of Brahman as *Rasa* or *Ānanda* has been interpreted to mean the unity in duality of the ultimate reality, the unity of *śakti* and the *śaktiman,* Rādhā and Kṛṣṇa finding fulfilment in each other. Since *Rasa* (relish) and *Ānanda* (bliss) have no meaning except as enjoyment which implies the duality of subject and object, the true nature of the ultimate reality is conceived as consisting of perfect self-enjoyment which finds its fullest and highest expression in the eternal communion of Rādhā and Kṛṣṇa. Numerous finites spirits and innumerable objects of experience are but imperfect manifestations of the perfect self-enjoyment of the ultimate reality. As *Rasa* (relish) the supreme reality is not only the object relished as bliss but also the subject that relishes. Kṛṣṇa, the supreme reality, is eternally engaged in relishing bliss either in the form of the bliss of His own self (*svarūpānanda*) or in that of the bliss of His own power or *sakti*(*Śaktyānanda*). His own bliss which is identical with *Hlādinī*, the highest aspect of His *Svarūpa-śakti,* becomes much more relishable to Him when reflected in the hearts of His devotees and associates. Thrown into the hearts of the devotees, *Svarūpānanda* (bliss belonging to the self) gets transformed into intense love known as *Bhakti* or *Prema* which is eagerly sought to be enjoyed by Kṛṣṇa Himself. This aspect of bliss exercising an intoxicating influence on Kṛṣṇa is termed *Śaktyānanda* and thought to be dearer to Kṛṣṇa than His *Svarūpānanda.* In the eyes of the devotees through whom He enjoys His own bliss as *śaktyādnanda* Kṛṣṇa appears as all-beauty and all-sweetness. The majesty of Kṛṣṇa ceases to exercise its influence on His devotees and associates who are His spiritual parts and remains simply to add to His all-round sweetness. Governed by a sense of

Kṛṣṇa-centred egoism (*Madīyatā*) as distinguished from the sense of dependence on Kṛṣṇa the citizens of the highest plane of spiritual experience (*Vraja*) display four different varieties of love which differ greatly in intensity. The attitudes mentioned in this system are (1) *Dāsya* (love of the ideal servant for the master), (2) *Sakhya* (love of a real comrade for another), (3) *Vātslya* (love of truly affectionate parents for their children) and (4) *Kāntā* (the intense love of a damsel for her paramour), of which every successive attitude is inclusive of and adding to the excellence of the previous one. Kāntā-bhava or the attitude of mad love like that of a girl for her lover, however, is the best, for it surpasses all the other attitudes in respect of sweetness and freedom. Love being essentially dynamic, the attitude involved in the love of a damsel for her paramour does not stop at a block lane, but continuously progress through the stages of *Sneha, Māna, Praṇaya, Rāga, Anurāga, Bhāva* and *Mahādhāva.* Various phases of this attitudes of unrestricted love flowing ceaselessly in all directions have been illustrated by the conceptions of *Gopīs* amongst whom Rādhā is the greatest. Love finds its culmination in Mahābhāba which is identified with Rādhā who is at once the source and fulfilment of all love. The different phases of love are included in Mahābhāva which infinitely trascends them. While Mahābhāva is identified with Rādhā, the less perfect manifestations of it are conceived as *Gopīs* who live in, for and by her in the transcendental realm of enjoyment. Though Rādhā is the highest ideal of perfect love, yet she is not complete by herself, for apart form relation to its object even the best of all love is a mere abstraction. Nor is Kṛṣṇa, the highest perfection of beauty and sweetness at whom perfect love aims, complete by himself, for beauty apart from love which discovers and appreciates it is altogether meaningless in the highest ideal of perfect love and the highest ideal of perfect beauty and sweetness, *Mahābhāva* and *Rasarāja,* Rādhā and Kṛṣṇa, are not exclusive of each other, but they are the two inseparable aspects of the integral reality which is a unity in duality and duality in unity. Expect as mirrored the Mahābhāva aspect of its power of bliss (*Hlādinī śakti*) the true nature of the ultimate reality is incapable of being completely known. Brahman intuited by the Advaitins who follows the path of Knowledge, and Paramātman realised by those who follow the path of Yoga, represent more or less partial manifestations of the ultimate reality which can be fully experienced only through the most perfect love of the ideal devotee. The highest conception of the ultimate reality is that of the eternal communion between *Mahābhāva* and *Rasarāja* at their best, between perfect love and perfect beauty fully realised, between Rādhā and Kṛṣṇa as revealed in Rāsa-lilā (*i.e.* amorous sport in the highest level of transcendental plane.)

Five

AN INTRODUCTION TO GAUDIYA VAISHNAVISM

The All-Embracing Doctrine of Divine Love of Sri Kṛiṣhṇachaitanya Mahaprabhu

Mangalacarana

vande 'ham sri-guroh sri-yuta-pada-kamalam sri-gurun vaisnavams ca
sri-rupam sagrajatam saha-gana-raghunathanvitam tam sa-jivam
sadvaitam savadhutam parijana-sahitam kṛṣṇa-caitanya-devam
sri-radha-kṛṣṇa-padan saha-gana-lalita-sri-visakhanvitams ca

"I offer my respectful obeisances unto the Lotus Feet of my Spiritual Master and unto the feet of all Vaishnavas. I offer my respectful obeisances unto the Lotus Feet of Srila Rupa Gosvami along with his elder brother Sanatana Gosvami, as well as Raghunatha Dasa and Raghunatha Bhatta, Gopala Bhatta, and Srila Jiva Gosvami. I offer my respectful obeisances to Lord Kṛiṣhṇa Chaitanya and Lord Nityananda along with Advaita Acharya, Gadadhara, Srivasa, and other associates. I offer my respectful obeisances to Srimati Radharani and Sri Kṛiṣhṇa along with Their associates Sri Lalita and Vishakha."

Vaishnavism Defined

"Vaishnavism" is the concept of Kṛiṣhṇa (also known as Vishnu) as God. More than that, it is the eternal relationship between the *jivatmas* (individual living entities) and the Eternally Self-Existing, Self-Luminous and All-Pervading Supreme Lord, Sri Kṛiṣhṇa. "Gaudiya" (pronounced Gauriya) Vaishnavas trace the origin of their tradition back through time to Kṛiṣhṇa Himself who declares boldly in *Srimad Bhagavad-gita* (10.8):

aham sarvasya prabhavo
mattah sarvam pravartate
iti matva bhajante mam
budha bhava-samanvitah

"I am the source of all spiritual and material worlds. Everything emanates from Me. The wise who perfectly know this engage in My devotional service and worship Me with all their hearts."

Lotus-eyed Sri Kṛiṣhṇa revealed His Divine Nature to His disciple, Brahma, the first embodied being and co-creator of the material universe. Brahma, in turn, instructed his disciple Narada who then taught it to Vedavyasa, the compiler of the Vedas, the sacred scriptures of ancient India. This divine knowledge was eventually explained by the great Vaishnava saint, Madhavacharya (approximately 1238-1317). In the year 1486, All-Merciful Sri Kṛiṣhṇa appeared as Lord Chaitanya Mahaprabhu to deliver the fallen souls in the present age of Kali (explained below). This same spiritual truth is now being disseminated to the four corners of the earth by the contemporary Vaishnava *acaryas* (those who teach spiritual knowledge by means of personal example).

evam parampara praptam
imam rajarsayo viduh

"This supreme science was thus received through the chain of disciplic succession and the saintly kings understood it in that way" (Bhagavadgita, 4.2).

Gaudiya Vaishnavism takes its title from the word "*Gauda*" (pronounced "Gaura"), the former name of the state of Bengal, India. Gaudiya Vaishnavas are those who follow the teachings of Sri Kṛiṣhṇa-Chaitanya Mahaprabhu, Who chose the state of Gauda to be the place of His appearance on *Bharata-varsa* (the earth planet). The advent of Sri Kṛiṣhṇa in the form of Lord Gauranga (Lord Chaitanya) is established by the *Bhagavata Purana* (11.5.32), wherein it is said:

kṛṣṇa varnam tvisakṛṣṇam
sangopangastra-parsadam
yajnaih sankirtana-prayair
yajanti hi su-medhasah

"In the age of Kali, intelligent persons peform congregational chanting to worship the incarnation of Godhead who constantly sings the names of Kṛiṣhṇa. Although His complexion is not blackish, He is Kṛiṣhṇa Himself. He is accompanied by His associates, servants, weapons and confidential companions."

One of the greatest Vaishnava scholars, Srila Jiva Goswami, has elucidated the meaning of this Sanskrit *sloka* (verse) in his work, *Krama-Sandharbha.* In this literature, he states that Lord Kṛiṣhṇa also appears with a golden complexion. In the *Srimad-Bhagavatam* (*Bhagavata Purana*), Garga Muni says that although the child Kṛiṣhṇa was blackish, He also appears in three other colors, red, white, and yellow. The colors of these different avataras (the assuming of different forms by Lord Kṛiṣhṇa when He descends into the innumerable material universes) correspond to the different divisions of material time known as the four *yugas*: *Satya-yuga* (white), *Treta-yuga* (red), *Dvapara-yuga* (black), and lastly, the present era, or *Kali-yuga* (yellow), which began approximately five thousand years ago, and is scheduled to last a total of 432,000 years. These divisions are similar to the golden, silver, bronze and iron ages of Western culture.

Lord Chaitanya is known as "*Gauranga*" which means "possessing a golden (or yellow) colored body." "*Kṛṣṇa-varnam*" means repeating or uttering the syllables "*Krs-na*". This implies that Gaudiya Vaishnavas can immediately be recognized by group or congregational chanting of the Lord's Holy Names. Lord Chaitanya Mahaprabhu, who is Lord Sri Kṛiṣhṇa Himself, personally divulged this sublime process of *sankirtana*, or chanting the Divine Names of God by means of the "*Mahamantra*" ("the greatest of all *mantras*"):

Hare Kṛiṣhṇa, Hare Kṛiṣhṇa, Kṛiṣhṇa Kṛiṣhṇa, Hare Hare,

Hare Rama, Hare Rama, Rama Rama, Hare Hare

Sri Kṛiṣhṇa's appearance as Lord Chaitanya is also confirmed in the *Visnu-sahasra-nama* ("the thousand names of Vishnu") from chapter 189 of Dana-dharma-parva *of the* Mahabharata:

suvarna-varno hemango
varangas candanangadi

"In His early pastimes He appears as a householder with a golden complexion. His limbs are beautiful, and His body, smeared with the pulp of sandalwood, seems like molten gold."

Basic Tenets of Gaudiya Vaishnava Philosophy

Bhaktivinode Thakur, the pioneer of the present movement of Sri Chaitanya Mahaprabhu's Doctrine of Divine Love (1838-1914) has stated that, according to Lord Chaitanya Himself, the Vedas teach nine principal doctrines. Listed below are these nine doctrines, followed by explanations of these points based upon the commentary of Thakur Bhaktivinode.

1) Hari, or Kṛiṣhṇa, is One without a second. We are perhaps accustomed to seeing in so-called Hinduism a trinity of gods, Brahma, Vishnu and Shiva. These three are the controllers of specific potencies or energies (saktis) respectively

known as sattva, rajas and tamas. Vishnu controls sattva-guna or "the mode of goodness" (the sustaining principle), Brahma controls rajo-guna or "the mode of passion" (the creative principle), and Shiva controls tamo-guna or "the mode of ignorance" (the destructive principle). Many other demigods occupy the Hindu pantheon. The elephant-headed god Ganesha and goddess Kali or Durga figure very prominently. Brahma and Shiva have expanded from Vishnu (Kṛishṇa), and ultimately, all other demigods and demigoddesses are but aspects of the One Supreme Person. In Bhagavad-gita (7.7), Sri Kṛishṇa Himself states assertively:

mattah parataram nanyat
kincid asti dhananjaya
mayi sarvam idam protam
sutre mani-gana iva

"O conquerer of wealth, there is no truth superior to Me. Everything rests upon Me, as pearls are strung on a thread." Again, in Bhagavad-gita (5.29), Lord Kṛishṇa also says:

bhoktaram yajna-tapasam
sarva-loka-mahesvaram
suhrdam sarva bhutanam
jnatva mam santim rcchati

"A person in full consciousness of Me, knowing Me to be the ultimate beneficiary of all sacrifices and austerities, the Supreme Lord of all planets and demigods, and the benefactor and well-wisher of all living entities, attains peace from the pangs of material miseries."

Analogous to the Hindu trinity, three stages of realization of God are described in the Vedic literature, i.e., Brahman, Paramatma and Bhagavan. This concept is similar to the Holy Trinity found in the Christian Church. Brahman is that aspect of God which is impersonal and featureless, devoid of categories. It is, in other words, without form.

Paramatma is that aspect of God where His full form is only partially manifested to the observer. Bhagavan or Kṛṣṇa-Bhagavan is the revelation of Sri Kṛiṣhṇa as He is, complete, fully formed with all paraphernalia and entourage as described by Lord Brahma in Brahma-samhita (5.29-30):

cintamani-prakara-sadmasu kalpa-vrksa-
laksavrtesu surabhir abhipalayantam
laksmi-sahasra-sata-sambhrama-sevyamanam
govindam adi-purusam tam aham bhajami

venum kvanantam aravinda-dalayataksam
barhavatamsam asitambuda-sundarangam
kandarpa-koti-kamaniya-visesa-sobham
govindam adi-purusam tam aham bhajami

"I worship Govinda (Kṛiṣhṇa) the primeval Lord, the first progenitor who is tending thecows, yielding all desire, in abodes built with spiritual gems, surrounded by millions of purpose trees, always served with great reverence and affection by hundreds of thousands of laksmis or gopis. I worship Govinda (Kṛiṣhṇa), the primeval Lord, who is adept in playing on His flute, with blooming eyes like lotus petals, with head decked with peacock's feather, with the figure of beauty tinged with the hue of blue clouds, and His unique loveliness charming millions of Cupids."

An analogy can be given to illustrate Hari or Kṛiṣhṇa's unique position. Imagine that you are approaching a mountain range. All that one can see from afar is one, amorphous mass. This is analogous to the experience of Brahman. Definable form is not yet visible. As one draws closer, individual peaks become noticeable. This is analogous to the experience of Paramatma. Partial form is now visible. Finally, when one is in the immediate vicinity of the mountain range, all details are visible such as the types of vegetation and animals on the sides of the mountains. This is analogous to the experience of Bhagavan, Who is Karana-karanam (the Cause of all causes) and the source of all objects of sense perception. As far as the relationship between the soul and Sri Kṛiṣhṇa is concerned, "distance" is not a time-space concept, but rather, a psychological state of intensity of concentration, or lack thereof. In common parlance, if someone were to say, "You seem 'distant'," it would imply that one's mind was "somewhere else." The disease of the soul is forgetfulness of God. It is our life's duty to focus our attention one hundred percent upon Kṛiṣhṇa—the Supreme.

(2) Kṛiṣhṇa is always vested with infinite power. Kṛiṣhṇa, or God, is ultimately powerful. No one is equal to, or greater than Him. His will is supreme. His will is so powerful that even though He is the Creator of all things, including time and space, He is not bound by the laws which govern His creations. Without Sri Kṛiṣhṇa's mercy, one cannot even pray to Him for mercy. This is His unique position. Being absolute, He (the Divine Person) and His Divine Name (*i.e.*, that sound which describes Him perfectly) are one and the same. For example, when one utters the word "water" in the mundane world, no matter how thirsty one is, no quenching of thirst is obtained. The real water exists separately from that sound which describes it. God, being absolute, (that is to say, being all things), means that when His Holy Name is uttered, He is non-different from that sound. In other words, He is factually present. His name is not a mere symbol or representation. A word is not true unless it is identical with the object it describes. Truth means perfect, complete. Any symbol is intrinsically imperfect and incomplete. Sri Kṛiṣhṇa's infinite potency is wholly invested in His Name and one who utters it with complete devotion and a submissive attitude will become attracted to Him and lose all attraction for worldly affairs.

giram asmy ekam aksaram
yajnanam japa-yajno 'smi

"Of vibrations I am the transcendental om. Of sacrifices I am the chanting of the holy names (japa)," Bhagavad-gita (10.25).

(3) Kṛiṣhṇa is the Ocean of Rasás. The Supreme Personality of Godhead is the source of all types of relationships and all possible emotional/psychological states. In the ancient Sanskrit language, relationships or more specifically, the different moods which prevail between God and the individual living entities, are known as rasas. There are five main rasas which are ultimately spiritual in nature, but due to the influence of the soul's association with matter, are perceived in an incomplete, and hence distorted way. They are as follows: *santa* (neutrality), *dasya* (servitude), *sakhya* (friendship), *vatsalya* (parenthood), *madhurya* (lover/beloved). That Supreme Person who is infinitely expressive by nature has also granted each sentient being the ability to be expressive. Free will means the freedom to express oneself without obstruction or interference. When the natural tendency to love God is diverted by interest in mundane material affairs due to misuse of free will, then one engages in the preceding five types of relationships with a sometimes conscious, sometimes unconscious attitude of exploitation. Instead of acting in a giving and serving manner, we wrongly think that we are the master of all that we survey. As a result, discord inevitibly results between employer and employee, friend and friend, parent and child, and also between husband and wife. The real self or atma is actually meant to serve Kṛiṣhṇa eternally in the spiritual world (Vaikuntha: where there is no anxiety or discord). Only persons can engage in relationships, and God is a person, as He Himself confirms in Bhagavad-gita (15.19):

yo mam evam asammudho
janati purusottamam
sa sarva-vid bhajati mam
sarva-bhavena bharata

"Whoever knows Me as the Supreme Personality of Godhead, without doubting, is the knower of everything. He therefore engages himself in full devotional service to Me, O son of Bharata."

Personal conscious beings exhibit the propensity to interact with each other with the aim of achieving happiness. A man or a woman expands into two by means of marriage to find happiness. Failing in this endeavor, they attempt to increase their happiness by begetting children. When these children grow up, they may also have their own children, making the original husband and wife grandparents, and so on. By continually increasing the quantity of family members, happiness still eludes them. Even if the entire population of the planet were to unite as one, still, without Kṛiṣhṇa there would be no happiness. The final object of relationships or rasas is God. Kṛiṣhṇa is known as *akhila-rasamrta sindhu* or the "ocean of nectar of the entire body of rasas." This subject has been commented upon very nicely by the great Vaishnava scholar Srila Rupa Goswami in his book, Bhakti-rasamrta-sindhu ("the nectar which is derived from the ocean of devotion").

(4) The soul is Kṛiṣhṇa's vibhinnamsa, or separated part. In the Vedic literatures that element which determines the difference between a dead thing and a living thing is known as atma. The atma is described as a minute particle of spiritual energy. The example is given of the sun with rays of light emanating from it. God is like the orb of the sun while the infinite individual souls are like atomic portions of the rays of the sun, dependent upon their source for existence. Usage of the word "portion" in this example should not create an impression of a chip cut by an axe but rather, the example of one candle lighted from another. The first candle does not lose anything in the process. Infinity plus infinity equals infinity; infinity minus infinity also equals infinity. Atma, or the soul, is not exclusive to the human bodily form. The soul is not in time and space;

rather, it is completely spiritual and as such, can occupy different types of material bodies including plants and animals. No animation would be possible without the presence of atma or soul. This is explicitely stated in Sri Kathopanisad (3.3)

atmanam rathinam viddhi
sariram ratham eva ca

"Know the atma or jiva to be like one seated upon a chariot, and the body to be the chariot itself."

The Bhagavad-gita (15.8-9) further states:

sariram yad avapnoti
yac capy utkramatisvarah
grhitvaitani samyati
vayur gandhan ivasayat

srotram caksuh sparsanam ca
rasanam ghranam eva ca
adhisthaya manas cayam
visayan upasevate

"The living entity in the material world carries his different conceptions of life from one body to another as the air carries aromas. Thus he takes one kind of body and again quits it to take another. The living entity, thus taking another gross body, obtains a certain type of ear, eye, tongue, nose and sense of touch, which are grouped about the mind. He thus enjoys a particular set of sense objects."

A jiva in a human body has the ability to utilize his intelligence for the discernment of spiritual truth leading to the service of God. On the other hand, an animal or plant does not think much beyond eating, sleeping, mating, and defending. If human intelligence is not utilized for its correct function, then a bodily form without that necessity or ability will be acquired. For example, if one experiences some sort of medical problem for which one is bedridden for a prolonged period of time, or if one is an astronaut who has been in a weightless condition for some time, he will find that his leg muscles have atrophied, making it difficult, if not impossible, to walk. Likewise, when intelligence atrophies or becomes weak due to improper use (*i.e.*, using the intellect to engage in those activities not sanctioned by the Supreme Lord), an animal or plant body becomes more suitable to carry out the activities of the jiva. There is nothing unjust in this concept. The human form is only achieved after travelling through 8,400,000 species of life, indeed it is a rare gift. Where there is evolution there is the possibility of devolution. What goes up can come down. The atma, being "sat" (eternal), is forever an individual, able to interact with Kṛiṣhṇa. Never does the soul become one with God as some theories proclaim. Is it more desirable to taste sugar or to become sugar? To become sugar would remove the experience of taste. Satisfaction is in the act of tasting.

(5) Certain souls are engrossed by Prakrti, or the Lord's illusory energy. The natural or constitutional position of the spirit soul is that of God's servant. Sometimes, however, the desire to imitate or to act like God enters the heart. When this occurs, the soul in a state of ahankara (false egoism) becomes attracted by the powerful external potency of God, known as maya (literally meaning "not that", or in other words, "illusion"). Wrongly thinking himself to be the controller and the sole focus of attention, the deluded atma becomes trapped by the intricate, forever changing web of matter. The spirit soul is an eternally existing, conscious entity who is qualitatively, but not quantitatively, the same as God. In the Sanskrit language, the body of Kṛiṣhṇa and that of the jivatmas or other living beings is described as "sat-cit-ananda." Atma is sat (eternal), matter is asat (non-eternal); atma is cit (knowledgeable), matter is acit (ignorant); atma is ananda (blissful), matter is nirananda (without bliss). It does not take a great leap of imagination to understand that these two items (atma and matter) are, in principle, incompatible.

The material casing which surrounds the jivatma is composed of eight elements. They are, from the grossest to the most subtle: earth, water, fire, air, ether, mind, intellect, and false ego. Ahankara, or false ego, means that one has identified himself with dull, insentient matter. This misidentification is the cause of three types of suffering: *adi-atmika* (afflictions caused by our own body), *adi-bhautika* (afflictions caused by other living beings), and finally, *adi-daivika* (afflictions caused by natural disasters). A description of the relationship between maya and the jiva is given in the following example. In the desert, when it is very hot, there appears to be water off in the distance, but when we approach it, we find it to be an illusion, a mirage. As we get closer, it seems to recede into the distance. We never reach the phantom water. The world of matter is just that—a mirage, nothing more. It promises, but never delivers. Therefore, a wise person will come to the conclusion that one should utilize one's valuable human life for its intended purpose, to serve and love God, rather than chasing after transitory material things such as wealth, beauty, fame, etc. In this regard, Lord Kṛiṣhṇa advises us in Bhagavad-gita (7.14):

daivi hy esa guna-mayi
mama maya duratyaya
mam eva ye prapadyante
mayam etam taranti te

"This divine energy of Mine, consisting of the three modes of material nature, is difficult to overcome. But those who have surrendered unto Me can easily cross beyond it."

(6) Certain souls obtain freedom from the grip of Prakrti. Kṛṣṇsika-sarana, or surrender to Lord Kṛiṣhṇa, is the only means of crossing over the ocean of birth and death (samsara). Performance of one's duty, simple morality, development of bodily or mental powers, acquisition of material knowledge, detachment from material things, or even the knowledge that one is a spiritual being cannot bring about realization of God. Vision of God is proportionate to the degree of bhakti or love for Him in one's heart. Lord Kṛiṣhṇa says in the Bhagavad-gita (18.55):

bhaktya mam abhijanati
yavan yas casmi tattvatah
tato mam tattvato jnatva
visate tad-anantaram

"One can understand Me as I am, as the Supreme Personality of Godhead, only by devotional service. And when one is in full consciousness of Me by such devotion, he can enter into the kingdom of God."

To possess bhakti or love for God means to have come in contact with a vaisnava—a lover of God. This comes about due to sukrti or past tendencies towards spiritual culture. If one holds ice near one's body, he becomes cold. If one holds a flame near one's body, he becomes hot. If one associates with a devotee—a vaisnava—he becomes devoted to God. Prahlada Maharaja was a great devotee who, when he was only a young boy, spoke of nine processes which, if executed with sincerity, are sure to reinstate one's original position as an eternal servitor of the Lord. He says in the Srimad-Bhagavatam (7.5.23-24):

sravanam kirtanam visnoh
smaranam pada-sevanam
arcanam vandanam dasyam
sakhyam atma-nivedanam

iti pumsarpita visnau
bhaktis cen nava-laksana
kriyeta bhagavaty addha
tan manye 'dhitam uttamam

"Hearing and chanting about the transcendental holy name, form, qualities, paraphernalia, and pastimes of Lord Visnu, remembering them, serving the lotus feet of the Lord, offering the Lord respectful worship with sixteen types of paraphernalia, offering prayers to the Lord, becoming His servant, considering the Lord one's best friend, and surrendering everything unto Him (in other words, serving Him with the body, mind, and words) these nine processes are accepted as pure devotional service. One who has dedicated his life to the service of Kṛishṇa through these nine methods should be understood to be the most learned person, for he has acquired complete knowledge."

(7) All spiritual and material phenomena are the Acintya-bhedabheda-prakas (tattva) of Hari, or Kṛishṇa, the Almighty. Everything that could possibly be perceived is emanating from the Supreme Personality of Godhead, Sri Kṛishṇa. We are informed of three general divisions of the potency of Kṛishṇa. The sastras (scriptures) describe them as follows: hladini-sakti (the spiritual realm), jiva-sakti (the individual living entities), and lastly, maya-sakti (the deluding potency of the illusory world of matter). Kṛishṇa's energies are the same as Kṛishṇa Himself and yet simultaneously they can be discerned to be distinct from Him. This is technically known as "acintya-bhedabheda-tattva" or "inconceivable, simultaneous distinction/ non-distinction." This concept is very accurately conveyed in the invocation to Sri Isopanisad:

om purnam adah purnam idam
purnat purnam udacyate
purnasya purnam adaya
purnam evavasisyate

"The personality of Godhead is perfect and complete, and because He is completely perfect, all emanations from Him, such as this phenomenal world, are perfectly equipped as complete wholes. Whatever is produced of the Complete Whole is also complete in itself. Because

He is the Complete Whole, even though so many complete units emanate from Him, He remains the complete balance."

As stated previously, there is a popular notion that the Supreme Personality of Godhead is not the Ultimate Cause of all causes. Contrary to sastric evidence, and common sense, this pseudo-theory states that Brahman (formlessness) is the impetus for the existence of Bhagavan (Sri Kṛishṇa, Who is Himself, the Ultimate Form). However, that which possesses form comes from that which also possesses form. Something cannot come from nothing. For instance, one comes from one's parents, and they in turn are born of their parents and so on. It is not logically consistent with the observable facts to arbitrarily state that, somewhere back in time, form comes from that which is formless. Conscious, animate beings come from other conscious, animate beings. Form is produced by consciousness. The idea of personality is integral to the idea of consciousness. For example, when one hears a piece of music, one does not think that the particular arrangement of notes and rhythms has come about accidentally. Rather, one knows it to have been produced by a thinking, willing being. Even a child would think this to be true. In fact, the subtle nuances contained in the arrangement are nothing if not the reflections of individual characteristics of personality. Similarly, if one were to take a watch apart, (bearing in mind that the constituent parts, themselves, have already been manufactured by a conscious entity), then we were to put these parts in a box, close the lid and then shake the box, would the parts reassemble and become a watch? A sober person will surely see the point of this example. All things, including the concept of formlessness, are due to Kṛishṇa's will and Kṛishṇa's will alone. Kṛishṇa is all things and yet He simultaneously exists apart from them. God does not undergo any process of modification, that is to say, He is not influenced by His own potency of maya or illusion. He is always Isvara, or the controller of that potency. He is never deluded.

(8) Bhakti, or devotion to Kṛiṣhṇa, is the only means of attaining the final object of spiritual existence. Acts or works which are executed with the desire to obtain results for oneself are known as karma. Acts which are directed toward God without desire for results for oneself are known as bhakti. Good works, in and of themselves, will not be sufficient to bring about realization of God. However, when performed with the intent to serve God, then He can be realized. Likewise, jnana (cultivation of knowledge), in and of itself, will not reveal God. The cultivation of knowledge aligned with the desire to serve God will bring about realization of Him. If one proclaims himself to be a Hindu, a Muslim, a Jew or a Christian, these things can be changed. By altering one's mode of dress, language or rituals, a Muslim can become a Christian, etc. However, the essential element which lies at the root of these different faiths is devotion to God. Whether one is a Hindu, a Jew, or whatever, to claim to be religious must surely mean that one is a servant of God. This fact cannot be changed. In Sanskrit this is known as sanatana-dharma. Sanatana means "eternal" and dharma, in this context, means "that activity which is intrinsic to one's very existence," just as heat is an intrinsic quality of fire. What is the nature of that activity? That one is eternally serving. Service is not something we can choose to do or not do. Where is the living being who is not serving? One serves one's employer, one's parents, one's children, husband, wife, pets, and even inanimate things such as cars, etc. From birth to death, service is there. The choice which we can make, however, is who or what is to be the object of our service. Kṛiṣhṇa is the only true object of service. Kṛiṣhṇa is eternally existing and the jivatmas are also eternally existing. The relationship between them is also eternally existing. Bhakti, or sanatana-dharma, is the link between God and His devotees. Love of God is independent of caste, color, or creed. Sincerity of heart is the only requirement. Bhagavad-gita (18.66) states:

sarva-dharman parityajya
mam ekam saranam vraja
aham tvam sarva-papebhyo
moksayisyami ma sucah

"Abandon all varieties of religion and just surrender unto Me. I shall deliver you from all sinful reactions. Do not fear."

(9) Prema, or love of Kṛiṣhṇa, alone is the final object of spiritual existence. Kṛṣṇa-prema or complete and utter absorption in God is the ultimate siddhanta (conclusion) of Gaudiya Vaishnava philosophy. Nothing short of this would satisfy a bonafide suddha-bhakta (pure devotee). Sometimes we see that people offer prayers or mantras (specific word formulas with special potencies) to the Supreme Lord with a mentality of mixed desires. For instance, one may worship God for some wealth, beauty, fame, etc. Generally, when one desires such things, one superimposes one's pre-conceived notions upon God, meaning to say that one thinks of God as being very wealthy and powerful. Although God is indeed the most wealthy and the most powerful, the predominance of this type of thinking tends to obscure Kṛiṣhṇa's most intimate, and ultimately most appealing, attribute (tattva)—that of sweetness. This inhibits one from obtaining the ultimate result, Kṛṣṇa-prema (love of God). One may also approach God in order to obtain mukti (liberation). Freedom from material miseries is also not the aim of life. The example is given as follows: If one is imprisoned for one reason or another, generally, upon release, one does not reenter society with any money or assets. Release from the miseries endured while imprisoned does not mean that we are rich. From this example, we can see that release from the material world would not necessarily bring about a state of happiness or satisfaction. Similarly, one who is in debt can have all his debts paid, but this would not make him a wealthy man. In either of the above cases, even a single dollar would be better than nothing at all. The fact is, the jivatmas are in debt. They are temporarily utilizing Kṛiṣhṇa's property for their own purposes. In other words, the body, and all things related to it, are essentially a loan from God. Due to the burden of this debt, the spirit soul has been evicted from his home, the spiritual world, into the prison house of material illusion (durga). Bhakti is the only means of alleviating this situation. In the same way, the desire for knowledge of material things, such as mathematics, medicine, anthropology, geology, etc. also does not ultimately bring about happiness. In fact, quite the opposite has occurred. There is now pollution, ozone depletion, the destruction of entire species of fauna and flora, and the threat of wholesale nuclear war. Atma-nivedanam, complete and total surrender to the Supreme Lord Sri Kṛiṣhṇa in a mood of spontaneous, loving devotion is the only thing which will satisfy the cravings of the soul. The different processes for obtaining Kṛiṣhṇa recommended in the sastras are not given up when realization of His Most-Beautiful Form has been obtained; but rather, this experience serves only to increase the intensity of those activities due to the ecstatic nature of that vision. In other words, bhakti is Kṛṣṇa-prema, Kṛṣṇa-prema is bhakti. It is both the means and the end. Kṛiṣhṇa is only satisfied by bhakti, and when Kṛiṣhṇa is satisfied, the entire universe is satisfied. In Sri Caitanya-Caritamrta (Adi-lila 4.166) the author, the great Vaishnava poet/saint, Srila Kṛiṣhṇadasa Kaviraja, has stated:

kamera tatparya—nija sambhoga kevala
kṛṣṇa-sukha-tatparya-matra prema ta' prabala

"The object of lust is only the enjoyment of one's own senses. But love caters to the enjoyment of Lord Kṛṣṇa, and thus it is very powerful."

Thus, in conclusion, it should be understood that nothing can be equal to or greater than love for Kṛiṣhṇa, the Supreme Person.

Vaishnava Devotional Practices, Arca-vigraha: Kṛiṣhṇa's

Deity Form. At this point, it may have come to the sagacious reader's attention that Vaishnavism very much emphasizes the concept of form as being a priori. This, as would be expected, also plays a major role in the methods of worship (bhajana) performed daily by a Vaishnava. Inside a Vaishnava temple or home you will find sri murtis (deity forms) of Lord Kṛishṇa. The unfamiliar Western reader, due to misinformation or cultural conditioning may be tempted to interpret this as idolatry. However, one should consider that there have been, throughout history, enlightened, saintly persons whose descriptions of the Beautiful Form of the Supreme Personality of Godhead conform to those given in sastra as a means of verification of legitimacy. Images of God whimsically fabricated in the minds of unscrupulous men, of limited intelligence, without regard to authentic scripture, are indeed idols. That person with true transcendental vision can clearly see the Supremely Spiritual Entity residing within what appears to be, to the materialist, mere stone or metal, etc. Vishnu (Kṛishṇa) means "all-pervading." Vishnu (as Paramatma or "Supersoul") is inconceivably occupying all spatial locations simultaneously. He is everywhere. He resides in all things without restriction (vasudevah sarvam iti). Srila Bhaktivinode Thakur says: "The world attracts you through your senses, and as long as you do not see God in the objects of your senses, you live in an awkward position which scarcely helps you in procuring your spiritual elevation." He further states, "If words can create an impression upon our thoughts, and a watch can indicate time, then why should not a picture or a figure inspire associations of higher thoughts and feelings with regard to the transcendental beauty of the Divine Personage?" Ultimately, what is the difference in the usage of a pencil to describe God and the usage of a chisel to the same end? If God is incarnate in words (scripture), then why can He not be incarnate three-dimensionally according to descriptions contained within those same scriptural words?

Prasadam: (literally "mercy") the offering of foodstuffs or other items to the Supreme Lord with devotion. Lord Kṛṣhṇa says in the Bhagavad-gita (9.27):

yat karosi yad asnasi
yaj juhosi dadasi yat
yat tapasyasi kaunteya
ta kurusva mad-arpanam

"Whatever you do, whatever you eat, whatever you offer or give away, and whatever austerities you perform—do that, O son of Kunti (Arjuna) as an offering to Me." (Arjuna: the great warrior personality to whom Kṛṣhṇa is speaking the Bhagavad-gita).

Vaishnavas do not accept anything until it has first been offered to the Deity. Before foodstuffs are offered to the Lord, they are referred to as bhoga (enjoyment). Once they have been offered with heartfelt prayer to the Lord, then they are understood to have been tasted by Him and are then known as prasadam or "mercy." The food has become blessed or sanctified, and we can make spiritual progress by partaking of Lord Kṛṣhṇa's remnants. Kṛṣhṇa, being absolute, can taste the food merely by glancing at it. For Him, one sense can perform the function of any other. In other words, He can taste with His eyes, see with His ears, and so on. An admittedly crude analogy can be given to illustrate this idea. A bat is known to utilize sonar, or the process of bouncing soundwaves off the surface of objects which then create a "visual" image of the objects. Depth perception, awareness of boundaries, etc., is made possible by the varying degrees of intensity and other characteristics of the reflections received by the ears of the bat. The bat is literally "seeing" by means of his sense of hearing. By means of this illustration, we can see that even in this world, the role of the senses is not so rigid as we might believe. God, not being subject to any of the limitations of this world, and being inconceivably more sophisticated than the bat or any other living entity, is not required to consume the offered foodstuffs by any visible or seemingly physical means. With regards to the nature of offerings He will accept, Kṛiṣhṇa states in the Bhagavad-gita (9.26):

patram puspam phalam toyam
yo me bhaktya prayacchati
tad aham bhakty-upahrtam
asnami prayatatmanah

"If one offers Me with love and devotion, a leaf, a flower, fruit or water, I will accept it."

Vaishnavas are vegetarian. First of all, as one can see from the preceding quote, Lord Kṛiṣhṇa does not sanction eating the flesh of animals (including fish) or eating of eggs. These items cannot be offered to Him. Kṛiṣhṇa is "suhrdam sarva-bhutanam"—the well-wisher of all living entities. Material existence implies feeding off one another in order to survive. As we must do this, then we should follow God's instructions regarding this matter. Vegetables are certainly sentient; however, most plants are not destroyed by taking their fruit, etc., and even a child can see the difference in the state of awareness of a cow, for instance, and that of even the most sophisticated plant. Ahimsa (non-violence) is one of the qualities of a devotee of Kṛiṣhṇa. The offering of foodstuffs is a very important devotional practice. It should be understood, however, that everything belongs to God; in fact, our very souls belong to Him. Therefore, we should always offer the results of any and all endeavors to Him. In this way, our minds will become purified and Kṛiṣhṇa will reveal Himself from within our hearts.

Sadhana: spiritual practices. Vaishnavas mark their bodies in twelve places (the most visible being the forehead/nose) with sandalwood mixed with a clay from a tirtha (holy place) where Lord Kṛiṣhṇa exhibited His pastimes five thousand years ago. These markings, collectively known as *tilaka*, are of a distinctive character. A "U"-shape descends down the forehead into a leaf shape on the bridge of the nose. The "U" symbolizes Vishnu, and the leaf symbolizes a sacred plant called *Tulasi*. Tulasi, also known as Vrnda, is a great devotee goddess who assumed the form of a plant to be near Kṛishṇa. This story can be found in the Padma Purana. These twelve marks are actually temples, and Lord Kṛishṇa is requested to kindly enter into each one by means of uttering His different names while touching each mark. Devotees also wear Tulasi-malas, or necklaces of beads made from the wood of the Tulasi tree, and her leaves figure very prominently in the offering of prasadam as decribed earlier. When entering a temple or one's home (which should also have the atmosphere of a temple), one must take off one's shoes at the door, and then show respect to guru (spiritual teacher; literally means "heavy" with knowledge) and deity by bowing down. One should always be freshly bathed (Vaishnavas generally bathe two to three times daily, and then immediately apply tilaka). *Sauca* (cleanliness or purity) is quintessential to a devotional lifestyle—purity of both mind and body. Vaishnavas also observe four regulative principles which serve to develop that purity: no eating of meat, fish or eggs (as mentioned earlier), no gambling, no intoxication of any kind, and no sexual relations outside of marriage.

There are also many days throughout the year held to be special in the mind of a Vaishnava such as the appearance and disappearance days of all gurus, *Janmastami* (Lord Kṛishṇa's appearance day), *Gaura-Purnima* (Lord's Chaitanya's appearance day), Ratha-yatra (the chariot procession of Kṛishṇa in His form of Lord Jagannatha), *Govardhana-puja* (celebrating the lifting of a mountain by the child Kṛishṇa) and *Ekadasi* (fasting days twice a month). A detailed discussion of the regulative principles and Vaishnava holy days is beyond the scope of this paper, but suffice it to say that it is the duty of the serious devotee to remove all things averse to the remembrance of the Supreme Lord and to cultivate, with enthusiasm, all things conducive to remembrance of Him.

Vaishnava names and modes of dress. All Vaishnava names signify Kṛishṇa or one of His intimate associates. Thus, when one hears the name of a Vaishnava, one either knowingly or unknowingly remembers Kṛishṇa. These names are followed by the appellations "dasa" (masculine) or "dasi" (feminine) which mean "the servant of." For example, "Kṛishṇa dasa" means "the servant of Kṛishṇa." Male devotees who are householders (grhasta) wear white clothing, while those who are leading a celibate lifestyle, either as students (brahmacari) or as a permanent way of life (vanaprastha and sannyasi) wear saffron colored clothing (a shade of orange). Women generally wear saris in many colors; widows wear white saris and often shave threir heads. Men generally, keep their heads shaved with a small tuft of hair known as a "sikha" retained at the top of the back of the head. It should be understood, however, that external appearances are secondary to that which lies within the heart. One cannot and should not imitate a bhakta (a devotee) by merely adopting these outer trappings without sraddha (firm faith in Kṛishṇa and all things related to Him).

Japa and sankirtana: Chanting the Holy Names of SriKṛishṇa. The practiceof sankirtana, or congregational chanting of the Holy Name by means of the Mahamantra was discussed in an earlier section of this paper. Chanting is possibly the most visible activity of a bonafide Vaishnava. Repeating the Mahamantra quietly, individually, on a rosary of one hundred eight beads made of Tulasi wood is known as japa. It was the express instruction of Sri Chaitanya Mahaprabhu Himself that a fixed number of "rounds" (recitation of a complete rosary) of chanting of the Names of the Lord be performed daily, usually sixteen, although many dedicated devotees chant much more. The great saint Haridas Thakur, a contemporary and devotee of Lord Chaitanya, was renowned as Namacarya ("the Divine Master of chanting the Holy Name") due to his chanting of not less than 300,000 Names of the Lord daily. Although volumes have been written on the subject of sankirtana and japa, which for obvious reasons cannot be explored fully here, the following sloka from the Brhan-naradiya Purana is of the utmost relevance: harer nama harer nama harer namaiva kevalam kalau nasty eva nasty eva nasty eva gatir anyatha

"In this age of Kali, there is no alternative, there is no alternative, there is no alternative for spiritual progress other than the Holy Name, the Holy Name, the Holy Name of the Lord."

The usage of repetition in the above verse as a means of emphasis is rare in Vedic literature, and should be taken to indicate, without a doubt, the paramount position of importance this method of attaining self-realization holds in this era, the Kali-yuga ("the age of quarrel"). As has been previously stated, the Holy Name of Sri Kṛiṣhṇa and Sri Kṛiṣhṇa Himself are inseparable, and therefore wherever the Holy Name is, so is Kṛiṣhṇa. Bhagavad-gita concludes with the following statement, which these most unworthy authors fervently hope the sincere reader will take to heart:

yatra yogesvarah krsno
yatra partho dhanur-dharah
tatra srir vijayo bhutir
dhruva nitir matir mama

"Wherever there is Kṛiṣhṇa, the master of all mystics, and wherever there is Arjuna, the supreme archer, there will also certainly be opulence, victory, extraordinary power and morality. That is my opinion" (18.78).

Bibliography

Bhakti Ballabh Tirtha Maharaj. Affectionately Yours (a collection of letters and articles). Calcutta: Sree Chaitanya Gaudiya Math, 1997.

Bhakti Ballabh Tirtha Maharaj. Transcendental Lecture Series, USA. Phoenix: GOKUL, 1997.

Bhaktisiddhanta Sarasvati Gosvami Thakur. Sri Brahma-Samhita. Los Angeles: Bhaktivedanta Book Trust,1985.

Bhaktivedanta Swami Prabhupada, A. C. Bhagavad-gita As It Is. Los Angeles: Bhaktivedanta Book Trust, revised ed., 1994.

Bhaktivedanta Swami Prabhupada, A.C. Sri Caitanya-Caritamrta. Los Angeles: Bhaktivedanta Book Trust, 2nd ed., 1996.

Bhaktivedanta Swami Prabhupada, A. C. Sri Isopanisad. Los Angeles: Bhaktivedanta Book Trust, 1974.

Bhaktivedanta Swami Prabhupada, A.C. Srimad-Bhagavatam, Cantos 1-10, v.1., Canto 10, vol. 2 through Canto 12 completed by disciples of the author. Los Angeles: Bhaktivedanta Book Trust, 1988.

Bhaktivedanta Swami Prabhupada, A.C. The Nectar of Devotion, The Complete Science of Bhakti-Yoga. Los Angeles: Bhaktivedanta Book Trust, 1974.

Bhaktivinode Thakur. Sree Chaitanya Mahaprabhu: His Life and Precepts. Calcutta: Sree Chaitanya Gaudiya Math (no date given).

Karnamrita Das Adhikari. Katha and Kena Upanishads. Washington, D.C.: New Jaipur Press,1989.

Article by Akincanadas and Lalitadas